Robert F. Carter

KAIKAKU: Ups & Downs

A Guide for Interim CROs and DIY Management Teams in SMEs.

www.tredition.de

© 2021 Robert F. Carter

Publishing and print:
tredition GmbH, Halenreie 40-44, 22359 Hamburg

ISBN
Paperback: 978-3-347-35045-8
Hardcover: 978-3-347-35046-5
e-Book: 978-3-347-35047-2

About the author and his company

Robert F. Carter has a college degree from Zurich University in economics, business administration and industrial psychology. After almost a quarter of a century as general manager of a variety of industrial production companies in Switzerland, Germany, Hungary, Malaysia, Vietnam and Mexico, he set up shop as a freelance business consultant and one-to-one executive coach when he turned 50. Robert met Marianna 30 years ago (parallels to Robin Hood and Lady Marian are coincidental but accurate). Soon thereafter marriage was proposed and accepted. They are both proud of their two sons, Daniel and Benjamin.

Robert's company, Coaching for ReThink GmbH, registered in Roggwil, Switzerland, aims to live up to its name by inducing, rekindling and encouraging new thought processes in its clients. At Coaching for ReThink we do not believe in the old adage that '*a rolling stone gathers no moss*', but instead believe that '*if you rest, you rust*'. Henry Ford said, '*Thinking is the hardest work there is, which is probably the reason why so few engage in it*'; having validated this through experience, here is what Coaching for ReThink stands for:

Coaching for ReThink's credo: '*We believe that nobody can be held responsible for the gender, country or colour of skin they were born into. We believe instead that everyone can be held responsible for the beliefs they nurture.*'

Coaching for ReThink's vision: '*We want people striving to simplify processes to achieve Flow$^©$.*'

Coaching for ReThink's mission: '*Our mission is to steadily progress towards our vision – an undertaking akin to the intersecting of parallel lines! But then: the journey is the reward.*''

In lieu of a foreword, an anecdote about belief

'A thousand words will not leave so deep an impression as one deed.' – Henrik Ibsen

Kaikaku (改革, Japanese for 'radical change') can also mean a return to one's core belief. Therefore, radical change should not be confused with radical renewal or something radically new. A true story will explain what I mean.

For nine years, I dabbled in a variety of esoteric lore – astrology, numerology, enneagrams, feng shui, reiki, etc. – and in the bygone days when the following story took place, I had the reputation of an expert in these unholy fields – unholy because the person this story tells you about had been an observing Roman Catholic for almost 50 years. It should not come as a surprise that we did not always see eye-to-eye. We respected each other's differing views on the world in general and, in particular, on spirituality, but we did not enthusiastically seek the company of the other, and when we met, beliefs were never the subject of our discussions.

Therefore, I was rather taken aback when she appeared at the door to my office, asked if I had a minute to spare and came in, closing the door behind her. Her red eyes revealed that she must have been crying, and she was not her usual, confident self. I offered her the seat in front of my desk and asked how I could be of help. She fought back tears unsuccessfully and dabbed her eyes with a well-used handkerchief while she extended a piece of paper towards me. To my relief, it did not look like her written resignation from the company's employ. Instead, it contained two dates. It was not hard to guess that the dates were birthdays. She took a deep, quivering breath and told me that she had been an observing Roman Catholic since her very early childhood, that she attended mass daily and that she would have to confess to her priest about consulting someone like me (at which point I could not suppress a diabolical smile, though it was lost on her as she was speaking to the triangular paper calendar on my desk) about the delicate matter she was about to reveal. I was intrigued, of course, and my eagerness to hear her story made me sit forwards on the edge of my seat. I habitually quip and joke about serious matters (for which I usually receive an exasperated sigh and a 'Will you never grow up?' from my wife, Marianna), but this time my inner voice ordered me to hold my sharp tongue in its scabbard and to listen carefully. The dates on the piece of paper were indeed birthdays: one was her husband's, and the other was that of her husband's newly acquired lover.

Anxiousness – that I would fail, but also that I may succeed in revealing something valuable – showed on her face when she asked me to render an analysis about the people behind the birthdates – people I had never even seen before. I gathered my wits and delivered, according to her, an impressively accurate description of the two people. Eagerness to learn more chased away the anxiousness on her face, and she asked me what I would recommend her to do.

'Bake a cake, buy a bottle of excellent wine and a bunch of flowers and pay the happy couple a visit in their love nest,'

was my spontaneous answer. It made me take a mental note to brush up on my diplomacy and to train my inner voice to hold tighter reins on my tongue. When what I had said sunk in, fire lit up in her eyes, and if eyes could kill, I would not be around to tell this story. Mainly to defuse the situation and to lessen my fear of being killed by a pair of severe-looking eyes, I asked rhetorically,

'One of the pillars of your religion is forgiveness, isn't it?'

Still shocked by the sheer nefariousness of my proposal, she barely managed to nod in agreement. In a half-hour monologue, I described to her what she would lose if she did not do as I had suggested: almost 50 years' worth of time attending mass and her authenticity as a Roman Catholic. The very essence of her entire belief system was at stake in this matter, and its survival depended on her decision. After I ended my verbal elaboration on the issue, we sat in complete silence for a considerable period of time. With both of us showing a great interest in the folded hands in our respective laps, she finally looked me in the eyes, said,

'Thank you, Mr Carter'

got to her feet and left my office. With absolute confidence that true believers are very rare on this planet, I soon dismissed the episode as a quaint interlude. Thus, I was rather astonished when about three weeks later, she again appeared in the doorframe of my office, entered, closed the door and occupied the chair in front of my desk with a radiant expression on her face, exclaiming with sparkling eyes,

'I did it!'

My face must have revealed my puzzlement, because, with a trace of annoyance, she added,

'What you suggested – I did it. I baked a cake, bought a bottle of wine and a bunch of flowers and visited them in their new home.'

My eyebrows shot up and I chided myself inwardly for shooting off my big mouth again. As a true Piscean should, she noticed my discomfort and said,

'No, no, don't worry, Mr Carter. Everything went well – very well, actually. They were, of course, somewhat suspicious and didn't want to believe in my good intentions and well wishes for their happiness, but after we had eaten the cake, drank the wine and talked for about three hours, everyone was glad that the situation had been defused in such an agreeable manner.'

Speechlessness is not my hallmark, but I could only nod and grin dumbly before awareness kicked in. I extended a hand and congratulated her on her superhuman achievement. She thanked me again for the 'somewhat out-of-the-ordinary piece of advice' and left my office as happy as a cricket.

Why did I tell this story and what's the *kaikaku* effect?

I am sure there are other people with such strong beliefs. The above story is to remind them of the importance of their being true to their credo even if they have to change radically to revert to it.

The *kaikaku*-effect in this anecdote is a positive one: I admit that the radical change is not obvious in above story. – When her husband confessed to cheating on her with his new flame, she chucked him out of their home using language that lengthened her next visit at her confessor's unduly. – Our spontaneous responses reveal our true beliefs. Therefore, her spontaneous reaction was in utter contradiction to her beliefs. – The radical change came about when she visited the flower shop to buy a bunch of forget-me-nots to her rival. With this radical change in her attitude her beliefs and actions became one.

It is hard enough to be in the middle of a crisis, but if it gets even harder – for example, with a wisecracking smart aleck, like an interim manager with an at-times-unbearable manner, turning up – it is a tremendous relief to be able to fall back on something familiar that once worked well. Thus, if you act according to your true and honest beliefs, you are authentic and in harmony with all your senses, your body and your essence – in short, with your entire being. To reach this state of holistic bliss is the ultimate objective of the *kaikaku* process.

This book is meant as a guide for small and mid-sized enterprise (SME) executives and interim managers. Its motto is the same I assigned to the CQO (Chief Quality Officer):

'*I am not a teacher, but an awakener*' – Robert Frost.

For easier readability, the male gender is used throughout the book.

Chapter 1

A crisis rarely comes out of the blue but is the result of negligence, lack of focus, and lack of discipline. – Almost all crisis can be prevented by daily practice of *hansei* (反省, Japanese for 'self-reflection') and *kaizen* (改善, Japanese for literally 'drive out the bad' but more usually translated into 'continuous improvement')

In a crisis *kaizen* is useless because its success lies in incremental, sometimes even imperceptible, changes in and to the system to forgo disruptions and stress caused by radical changes.

In a crisis *kaikaku* has to be applied to get back on track as soon as possible. – *Kaikaku* will also help you to introduce lean management. Which will prevent crisis any other than the ones due to vis major (like earthquakes, floods or pandemic diseases, etc.)

As I said, do not let the crisis go to waste but implement lean management quickly and efficiently. Why is a crisis a gate-opener for lean management? Because lean management thrives on simplicity, and established enterprises have usually developed some very complex systems that are hard to dismantle in a non-crisis situation but that can be discarded with the flick of an imaginary wand when existences are at stake. – Under chapter 11 ('reorganisation bankruptcy procedures' in the USA), and other similar regulations in other countries, a lot of *kaikaku* is done and hardly any *kaizen.*

Complex systems operate with a lot of manpower. Simple systems, on the other hand, run with far fewer people, or even autonomously. Therefore, resistance to change is much more contested in a non-crisis environment. Leaving the comfort zone out of one's own free will requires superhuman willpower – anyone who has tried to diet for any reason other than a medical one knows this. External forces furnish an excellent excuse to get long-overdue things done.

Having said that, it does not matter how severe a crisis is; the following, prevalent obstacles need to be overcome:

1) inner resistance -> only radical measures can break resistance;
2) slow learning -> triggering the instinct of survival speeds up learning; and
3) fast forgetting -> it is hard to forget a shocking experience.

Radical changes cause a lot of stress, therefore remind yourself of what Churchill had to say on changes might help to prevent crisis or at least to facilitate the implementation of change: *'We must take change by the hand or change will take us by the throat.'*

Implementing radical changes all by yourself is akin as pulling yourself out by your own bootstraps: extremely difficult and therefore hardly feasible. External help, like a 'friendly' kick in the butt should get you started. – Interim managers are professional 'butt kickers' and 'arm twisters', martinets really, who make you do what you have planned to do for a long time and never got around it. – If you have a martinet in your management team all you have to do is to vow to do whatever he says.

A word of caution to stakeholders and management:

do not use interim managers as stooges to implement your avowed solutions for mastering a crisis; you had ample time to do so before you hired external help! In the process of selecting an interim manager, look for the most impartial one. In the mid and long run, you do neither yourself, nor the company nor the selected interim manager any favours if you select someone to buttress your respective position. Usually, sticking to positions is what causes crises in the first place, because a battle of opinions (read: egos) can result in trench warfare where winning an argument becomes more important than saving the company.

That is why you should always have a BATNA (best alternative to a negotiated agreement, see 'Getting to Yes' by Roger Fisher and William Ury) ready so you do not sacrifice the company on the altar of oversized egos.

According to Seneca,

'If one does not know to which port one is sailing, no wind is favourable.'

Therefore, it is an excellent idea to define a key performance indicators (KPI) baseline at the very beginning of a project, regardless of the state of the company: progress has to be tracked and displayed for everyone to see. Brief progress reports, preferably using charts to show trendlines and going easy on verbose written explanations, are vital. Information about the current state is what everyone in a crisis wants. Nothing breeds malicious rumours more than a lack of information.

Choose a room – in lean management terminology also called an *obeya* (大 部屋, Japanese for 'big room') – where all teams involved in solving the crisis can congregate regularly to discuss the best way forward. Display the latest KPIs and catch up on what everyone has achieved so far.

A word of caution on Key Performance Indicators:

Always, and I do mean A L W A Y S, make sure you know where your figures come from, how they are compiled and how they are crunched before they get shown to the public. – Making sure is NOT just asking the controller whether he is happy with his data sources. – Making sure is to look for yourself by questioning even the tiniest detail about the data sources.

The power of figures is such that no matter whether they are true or false people tend to take them at face value and use them in their arguments.

I always try to make this room accessible to all employees because, as I have mentioned before, people crave information in a crisis. Letting them follow the progress helps to get them on your side – or at least prevents them from opposing you behind your back – by encouraging them to discuss matters openly. Keep everything as simple and as transparent as possible. Although it might sound outlandish but it is much easier to get to a complicated system than to a simple one. Why? Because the complicated system was not set up – it evolved usually by a series of well-intentioned quick-fixes. – But as we all know *'There is nothing so permanent than a temporary solution.'* – Milton Friedman

A simple system, on the other hand, is the result of simplification, which is an active process of making something easier. – During the entire journey out of the critical situation you have found yourself in, keep in mind Einstein's apt observation:

'If you can't explain it simply, you don't understand it well enough.'

The best way to explain something – anything really – is by visualisation. Visualisation is the most versatile and maybe also the most powerful tool in the lean management toolbox; use it extensively. Here, too much is better than not enough. Why? Because much like the child in Hans Christian Andersen's fairy-tale 'The Emperor's New Clothes' who pointed out that the emperor did not wear any clothes at all but was, in fact, totally starkers, it reveals everything and has no regard for status, politics, ideology or any other face-saving measures.

A word of caution on saving face:

No one likes to be blamed and shamed, especially publicly. However, in a crisis, all must be revealed so that problems can be solved as closely to their roots as possible. Psychology has extensively scrutinised people's associations and dissociations. Mentally sane people, a minority of the human beings, know exactly when they should associate with or dissociate themselves from events. Those prone to depression, like to associate themselves with negative events like:

'I am so unlucky. Of course, this has to happen to me after I've already lost my job, my car broke down and my partner walked out on me at the drop of a hat'

and dissociate themselves from positive ones

'A stroke of luck my foot! This only happened to lure me into a false sense of security that my ordeals are finally over.''

Those prone to megalomania do the opposite: they associate themselves with the tiniest success, whether they have been involved in creating it or not

'I and my team made it happen again! Where would they be without me?'

and dissociate themselves from failures

'How many times did I ask for XYZ to be removed from my team? They should have sacked them ages ago! No, they shouldn't have given XYZ a contract in the first place!' or *'My plan was perfect. Unforeseeable circumstances and the incompetence of some team members who I didn't select for this task have led to this failure, which could have been prevented if the powers that be had just listened to me.'*

That is why one of the three principles of *kaizen* is to not blame or shame anyone but to focus instead on the problem and ask 'why?' at least five times to find out the real reason. A conclusion about shame by Alexander Pope closes this short excursion:

'No one should be ashamed to admit he is wrong, which is but saying, in other words, that he is wiser today than he was yesterday.'

Decisions make or break success in times of crisis. The 'break' part is a certainty if no decisions at all are taken. There is no worse situation in a crisis than being in limbo because no decision has been made by the people in charge. Thus, all heads of departments have to decide on critically important issues on the spot. Standstills should be prevented at all costs because people become restless and listless quickly and easily. This can lead either to lethargy or to sedition – both are hard to handle. Therefore, it is better to let people march in the wrong direction and turn them around than leave them wondering what happens next. Having to keep order when nerves are frail because livelihoods are at stake or to rekindle spirits once despair has settled in is definitely not something you want as a manager when in a crisis; as Joan Baez had it,

'Action is the antidote to despair.'

A word of caution on management:

I encourage all managers to remind themselves that covering one's backside is a very short-term strategy. This is especially true in a crisis. Each and every manager who does not stand firm in the face of danger will be (best-case scenario) ridiculed or (worst-case scenario) loathed for such incompetent behaviour. Just remind yourself that even after more than a hundred years, the description of the British army in World War 1, 'lions led by donkeys', is still around. Managers' high salaries should reflect their ability and willingness to take on responsibility, not the size of their inflated egos. One of *kaizen*'s 10 core beliefs is humility or even 'servant leadership'. Why servant? Because managers have the power to remove obstacles so that their direct reports can use their own expertise to their full extent, thereby achieving overall success for the company. Your direct reports know that you are the boss, so you neither have to show nor tell them. Instead remember Albert Schweitzer's thought on leadership:

'Example is not the main thing in influencing others. It is the only thing.'

Chapter 2

Typical manufacturing companies waste space (factories, warehouses, offices, meeting rooms, etc.), lead time (handling times, non-process-induced buffer times, waiting times, storage times, etc.) and resources (manpower, material, energy, etc.) on a large scale. Space and lead time can usually be reduced without having to face strong headwinds. Headcount reduction is the trickiest part; therefore, the very first step is to make sure that the main objective of *kaikaku* – the people – is not out of sight. If you thought that the main objective of *kaikaku* would be money, please think again.

'*Enterprise of the people, by the people and for the people shall not perish from the Earth*' is what the late US President Abraham Lincoln would have said if he had been a business consultant working on restructuring and turnaround projects. Or to put it even more up to the point by quoting John Maynard Keynes, who said '*It is enterprise which builds and improves the world's possessions. If enterprise is afoot, wealth accumulates; if enterprise is asleep, wealth decays.*'

A lot is on stake if you fail to rescue the enterprise from collapsing. Therefore, take every precaution to prevent the stake- and shareholders from losing faith in you and your approach by:

1) Making sure the company's culture allows for *kaikaku*. An arch-conservative culture will never, ever change radically; it will go under rather than go yonder. You cannot win them all, so let this particular chalice pass you by.

2) *Nemawashi* (根回し, Japanese for 'preparing the ground for planting'), that is, coming to an agreement with the stake- and shareholders and making them see what really needs to be radically changed (which only coincidentally happens to be what they think needs to be changed). Some Caskie Stinnett-style diplomacy is needed in these situations: '*A diplomat is a person*

who can tell you to go to hell in such a way that you actually look forward to the trip.' A mutual consensus (or at least a mutual compromise) has to be written down in a master schedule, and the tasks should be broken down and allocated to the appropriate departments which will, in turn, cascade these further to each and every employee so that everyone can feel part of the taskforce team setting out to save the company. Such an agreement can also be required by law, for example in German companies, where workers' councils have many rights of co-determination; one of these rights deals with whether management can hire a lean management consultant and implement lean management.

3) Making sure that Human resources (HR) selects the right employees to be trained, sent into retirement and made redundant, even if it takes a great deal of discussion. Let your impartiality help HR to sort the chaff from the wheat. - You do not want to be caught in a rescue mission where you have to rescue the rescuers, do you?

4) Allowing for enough time to pass for the frequent explanations to settle in. Only people who have a good grasp of what is going to happen next will help you. Once the 'converted' are in the majority, things will run (almost) by themselves.

5) Not fooling yourself! Change takes time. Make it clear to impatient stake- and shareholders by having them write with their non-writing hand the following sentence: 'I'd like to withdraw £500 from my account, please.' Have them sign it (also with their non-writing hand), then ask them whether they think they would get the cash from a bank clerk who does not know them from Adam. If they are ambidextrous, make them write with their foot.

6) Making sure that with *hoshin kanri* (方針管理 ,i.e. policy deployment) the show gets on the road. As soon as everyone knows what needs to be done, follow one of the leadership principles of the Swiss army: 'Command, Check, Correct'.

How serious is the situation?

Once you have agreed with all participants on what needs radically changed, find out how fast you have to act to save the company. Below are three scenarios of a patient arriving at A&E after an accident; these scenarios work as comparisons for an enterprise in trouble. The first thing any patient arriving at A&E gets is an infusion to stabilise their circulation. Therefore, whichever scenario you find yourself in, the first step must be the evaluation and stabilisation of the internal logistics processes.

Should they be deficient, immediate action is required. One of my favourite approaches is the implementation of *mizusumashis* (みずすまし, Japanese for 'water spider'; they are experienced workers with an excellent eye for detail that are able to quickly grasp complex situations). Once you are sure that raw materials, work-in-process items and finished goods are moving merrily down the value stream from one station to the next, you should continue evaluating the condition of your patient/enterprise. Here are the aforementioned scenarios:

1) The patient is bleeding, but the wounds can be attended to without much ado → the company is losing money, but cash reserves are sufficient to conduct *kaikaku* in an orderly manner. Key decisionmakers should be aware of what needs to be done in what time frame and where. The CQO (Chief Quality Officer) should be present at all meetings, monitoring the implementation process meticulously and surveying the *kata* (型 or 形, Japanese for 'training' or 'coaching').

2) The patient is bleeding and panicking → the company is losing money fast and has a sizeable backlog of orders that have not been produced or delivered. Customers are threatening law suits. After a brief discussion with the interim manager or the Chief Restructuring Officer (CRO; or, by this stage, the new CEO), key decisionmakers should be asked to do what has been agreed upon in the master chart as soon as possible, without any further

discussions or delays. At least one member of the Quality Management department should always be by the side of the interim manager, waiting for instructions to write procedures, processes and work descriptions. If there is time for training employees and their supervisors (including C-level management), it should be done. Even at this stage, the people in charge should try to adhere to Alexander Pope's advice: '*Men must be taught as if you taught them not, and things unknown proposed as things forgot*'.

3) The patient is bleeding profusely, is apathetic, and a priest waits in the foyer to perform the last rites → the company has run out of cash, the suppliers, as well as the customers, have sued the company for damages caused, and the liquidator is assessing assets with the CFO. In this case, the interim manager/CRO has to divide his time between the factory and the office according to the needs of operations and of the banks, authorities, liquidators. Members of the Quality Management department should be assigned to every C-level manager in the company to make sure that the orders of the interim manager/CRO are immediately implemented. Feedback at this stage is vital. Quality Management department staff have a healthy feedback culture as have comptrollers.

Discussions and agreements about what to do and who should do it decrease logarithmically from scenario 1 to 3. Having said this, if and when scenario 3 is turned into scenario 2 or scenario 1, this process is reversed, thus turning the logarithmic curve into an exponential curve. To once again use the comparison of the patient in hospital, this means that once the patient is out of A&E, he starts questioning the further procedures of his recuperation by asking, for example, about the side effects of the blue, yellow and red pills he has to take to get better. Put plainly, as long as people are in deep shit, they will readily accept assistance to get out of their misery; as soon as they are out of the woods, they'll start to veto your suggestions.

Let's take a look at each scenario in reverse order. Why? Because if you successfully turn scenario 3 into scenario 2, the client usually wants you to navigate the vessel through the rapids until it reaches calmer waters. Remember, though, that usually does not mean always: clients and their employees might have had enough of you and your wiseacre ways and might even quote Professor Snape from the Harry Potter books when he calls Hermione Granger *an insufferable know-it-all*. Then again, the ultimate freedom in the world is the freedom to botch up your life as you please without having someone tell you that you are just doing that.

A word of caution to the client:

Most interim managers are capable of leading a company through scenarios 3 to 1, even of staying on for scenario 0, which would mean that the interim manager converts to a permanent, C-level employee. However, interim managers have their preferences: some need the adrenaline kicks offered by scenario 3 and are grossly annoyed that discussions with management, stake- and shareholders intensify on the way to scenario 1. Others are happy to get scenario 3 done as quickly as possible so that they can establish some sustainable measures that will keep the company out of harm's way, at least for a while. For best results, ask the interim manager where his preferences lie. They might even tell you beforehand because usually, these people chose this particular career path because they wanted to rid themselves of the political scheming often prevalent in companies.

Whichever scenario the company is in, here are some cure-alls that interim managers and DIY management teams can always apply:

1) Find solid ground in the quagmire of a company in crisis
2) Draw up a concise priority list with a company scope and not with a department scope
3) Demand self-discipline and prohibit procrastination form the participants

First, look for 'solid ground' (in both sense of the word: stable platform and your personal best field of expertise) to start at; the lower in the value stream this solid ground is, the better. Moving upstream has the advantage that you do not have to look for junk – you meet it head on. Shipping is an ideal place to start because this is the point where your value-added goods leave the factory. The best-case scenario at this point is for shipping's only task to be loading lorries provided by customers and handing over freight documents. If the shipping department also has to manage other things, like ordering lorries or looking for the best transport route, or even if it has its own fleet of lorries to deliver goods, things become trickier. Why? Because the solid ground just turned into a shaky ground. To elaborate, my assumption is, quite distrustfully, that no departments in the company operate to a high enough standard. Therefore, the less influence that any department has on a procedure or process, the better. Of course, in this example, I am assuming that the customer is better organised – but you have to believe in something working right, don't you? If shipping has too much elbow room to push orders to and fro, disaster can occur. In this instance, you should find your fix point at the last department in the value stream: after-sales. They cannot influence deliveries because the customer has already received the goods. If the customers are not amused about what they have received, ask the people in the after-sales department to give you the three most annoyed customers, and, just as a comparison, the happiest three customers. Start to make the annoyed customers happy again by swimming up the value stream and eliminating all the junk (quality issues, faulty orders, below standard raw materials, overly long buffer times and so on) that comes your way.

Now, the second panacea is to ask for or create a priority list. Hint: priority lists can be long, but they are never allowed to be broad. You can read more about priority lists later, but here is a brief summary. Priority lists must live up to their names; on top should be the most important to-do, followed by the second-most-important to-do and so on – it sounds simple enough, but priority lists can be hard to create. Take your time in preparing the priority list. Make sure that the priorities are the priorities of all departments, not just the priorities of the most vociferous department (such as the sales department). A priority list is neither a fleeting star nor a flash in the p(l)an: it is meant to last for at least (and here I sound revoltingly mellow) the top five priorities on your list (in my younger years I would have demanded 'the top 10'). Once a topic on the priority list has been completed the next highest priority moves onto this august position. There might be acceptable circumstances beyond the scope of your influence that force you to cease proceedings on your top priority; then, of course, you have to start with the next feasible item on the list. Having said that, make sure the circumstances are really beyond your scope of influence: procrastination is a willing bedfellow.

Finally, demand self-discipline and prohibit procrastination. Without tenacity, persistence and determination, you will fail. There are always 'good' reasons for giving up or giving in. Do not change course when the wind starts to blow harder. Without an unyielding determination to succeed where others might fail you will not be able to master the task ahead. After a while persistence and determination become contagious and you will get more and more helping hands. Once you reached the 'critical mass' – more people believe in the success of the undertaking than are certain of its failure – the momentum will carry you forward.

Although I find above three cure-alls to be a complete list, I debated with myself about whether to add a fourth, like 'leadership' – but that one is really hackneyed. As is 'coaching'… What I mean to say is: do whatever you do selflessly for the company and its grassroots employees. Try to share as much as possible not only of your expertise but also of your life experiences. Maybe the tenets of Dale Carnegie's *How to Win Friends and Influence People* can help you here. – It points out the importance of respect (address everyone by their name, let them voice their opinions without telling them that they are wrong, appreciate the contribution of others and so on) and encouragement (smile, appeal to the higher motives of task ahead, give people a good reputation they can live up to and so on).

Chapter 3

Procrastination is hardly ever advisable, but at this stage, it is lethal. Do everything that needs to be done, and accomplish it immediately. Self-esteem and self-confidence build success, and *'nothing breeds success like success does,'* as the American painter Bob Ross said.

Departments and their duties during *kaikaku* in scenario 3

3.1. The CEO/CRO (Chief Executive Officer/Chief Restructuring Officer) in scenario 3:

The CEO agrees to hand over almost all of his executive powers to the interim manager, or simply hands in his resignation. In most cases, the shareholders/liquidator will already have transferred them to the interim manager, appointing him as a CRO, and released the CEO from his duties. If he is still around, his job is to assist the interim manager in his efforts to save the company to the best of his abilities. For example, he should keep all external stakeholders at bay and/or, depending on whether his standing is better outside or inside the company, make sure that all department heads and employees stay as calm as possible during the perilous journey through unchartered and choppy waters. He is a sparring partner to the interim manager and works with him to find solutions for tricky problems because he is a source of historic data that the interim CRO will probably want access to. However, if the CEO cannot stand the heat, he should get out of the kitchen asap. If he sticks around only to cause trouble shareholders should remove him instantly.

A motto for the CEO/CRO:

'However beautiful a strategy, you should occasionally look at the results' – Winston Churchill.

Why did I choose this particular quote? Because when you're at the top of the food chain, it is easy enough to get carried away by your own magnificence – and it is even easier to start feeling like the pope is said to be: infallible. Thus, you should make sure you keep yourself grounded. Remember that along with your privileges as the Top Dog, you have at least the same number of obligations to fulfil if not more.

An anecdote about a CEO in a scenario 3 environment:

Doing one's master's bidding obsequiously has its not-so-unforeseen consequences. A small-sized transportation-cum-industrial-assembly company's main shareholder interfered constantly with the ways in which the general manager was conducting business, to the effect that the company was on the verge of insolvency. I was hired to save the company from imminent doom.

Let us remind ourselves of my definition of a scenario 3 patient: *'the patient is bleeding profusely, is apathetic, and a priest waits in the foyer to perform the last rites.'* Well, by the time I was called in to help, the situation was a step or two further down the road: the last rites had been applied and the coffin was leaning against the wall while the most faithful employees held vigil.

I was not amused; on the contrary, I was livid. Seeing tangible and intangible values disintegrate always gets my hackles up, and all the more so this time because I was under the impression that my client, who I had worked for before, had called me in on this to show me my limits. Healing is one thing. Resurrection is something else entirely.

I put the general manager of the transportation company through a KGB-like interrogation until I got even the tiniest morsel of background information about how this unseemly situation had come about. This resulted in the decision that the company had to be split into two parts, one rescuable and one hopeless. The hopeless part was sold to a much bigger competitor in the transportation industry – not for cash, but to allow manpower and business to be transferred to the rescuable part.

The competitor must have sent in his best people because the rescuable part of the doomed company started to tick over and gather speed a mere three weeks after the experts had taken over from the regular employees. All looked rosy in the garden once more, so the majority shareholder, feeling sorry for his servile general manager – or for whatever reason – renewed the general manager's contract and gave him a second chance to get it right. I had mixed feelings about this decision and spoke to both the shareholder and the general manager about it. They both reassured me, rather convincingly, that they had learned their respective lessons and vowed to conduct business in a totally different spirit. Ever the optimist, I wished them the best of luck and took my leave after the first successful resurrection in my career so far. Within two years, the rescued part of the company went bust and was shut down by the authorities for good. The reason? The majority shareholder kept interfering, and the general manager kept doing his master's bidding.

Why did I tell this story and what's the *kaikaku* effect?

Shareholders and CEOs, please heed my advice: split competencies, stick to the rules and don't interfere in each other's business. And here is some bonus advice for shareholders and CEOs, free of charge. To shareholders, I say: remember what Thomas Carlyle had to say about communication: '*I don't like to talk much with people who always agree with me. It is amusing to coquette with an echo for a little while, but one soon tires of it.*' With this in mind, select C-level managers with enough chutzpah to lead your enterprise. Or, if you cannot stop interfering with how your enterprise is managed, get into the driver's seat yourself.

And to CEOs and interim managers, I say: do not take on a job or assignment if your future employer has a track record of interfering in daily operations. My own worst experience with an interfering shareholder in daily business was when, as an interim general manager, I had to facsimile (yes, the internet was operational by that time, but this particular, octogenarian shareholder was not all too keen on such tripe) customer orders to the shareholder so that he could sign, stamp and fax them back to me for further processing.

The *kaikaku* effect in this anecdote is one up and one down. – On the upside the radical change to split the company resulted in a successful, smaller enterprise. – On the downside the protagonists involved, namely the shareholder and the general manager, could not radically change their behaviours which lead to inevitable doom. – For better sustainability change not only the enterprise but change also your attitudes.

3.2. The CQO (Chief Quality Officer) in scenario 3:

Quality managers usually have a good understanding of all the procedures and processes in a company because they almost always have to write these instructions themselves. Only in an ideal world are procedures, processes and work instructions written by the heads of the respective departments and just edited by a member of the Quality Management department. Because of this, they can put their virtual fingers right in the middle of the most serious wounds and are among the best sparring partners for an interim manager to fine-tune serious decisions with. During my career, I have not met many Quality Management heads who liked to take decisions, but all of them have always known the best way forward – if only management would listen to them! *'If at first you don't succeed, try doing it the way your wife told you'* – this quip could easily be adapted to fit this situation by changing 'wife' to 'CQO'...

A motto for the CQO:

'I am not a teacher, but an awakener' – Robert Frost.

Why did I choose this particular quote? Because a quality manager's task cannot be teaching since they cannot be experts in all functions of a company. Instead, they must be awakeners of department heads. It is essential that each and every member of the management team understands the importance and uses of quality management systems.

An anecdote about CQO in a scenario 3 environment:

The company I had the honour to be appointed to as interim CEO was in an unholy mess – it was a task tantamount to cleaning the Augean stables, and I was at a loss for where to start. I was unable to find a fix point to start from. My very first step when starting at a company is to peruse the annual financial reports of the past two to three years and to put the CFO through a third-degree interrogation. The second step is to let my intuition roam and decide what immediate measures need to be taken. However, this time, my intuition was mute.

Reading is a hobby of mine; I indulge daily. Having to read Quality Management manuals, procedures, processes and work instructions puts my love of reading to a severe test every time I have to delve into the netherworlds of Quality Management bureaucracy. I am a fervent admirer of well-oiled Quality Management systems, but it is a bit like the love for sausages: the taste is great, but people don't want to see how they're made. Thus, with some reluctance, but still at a loss for what else to do, I asked the CQO to pop by any time suitable for him (not necessarily meaning immediately) and to bring hard copies of the aforementioned documents with him. I am fully aware that these days, all documents are digitalised and then cross-referenced and commented on, and that even the comments are hyperlinked. Having said this, my generation likes to scribble on a piece of paper – even if it is less efficient than keying the remarks into a computer program. - Nobody is perfect, and I do not want to be nobody!

To my chagrin, the CQO walked into my office a few minutes after I had finished my phone call with him. I did not fail to notice the stack of papers he was carrying under his arm, and thought, '*Well, asking for hard copies didn't delay him. This could be interesting*' – and it was. Never in my illustrious career have I encountered a better-prepared CQO or seen more perfect Quality Management documents than the ones I was introduced to over the next four hours. Duly impressed, I asked him how it was possible to have such a mess in the company with such an outstanding Quality Management system.

He replied, 'This company ran like a Swiss watch: we had stable processes, well-trained staff and due to these healthy profits. – So, what had happened? – The shareholders got greedy and demanded more profits. The CEO in those days was reluctant to take incalculable risks, thus, he got sacked and Mr X, your predecessor, got appointed. – Mr X said that Quality Management is about claims. Claims involve expenditures. Expenditures are bad for profit – therefore, Quality Management is bad, and I should stay as far away from him as possible.'

I thought I had heard all the stupid drivel about the uselessness of Quality Management in the trade, but this made my jaw drop. 'Yep!' exclaimed the CQO cheerfully, adding, 'That was Mr X's opinion about Quality Management. By the way, he delivered his aforementioned opinion during his inauguration speech, addressed to management and employees.'

I was suitably captivated: an announcement of such magnitude by the head honcho would have had the effect of a nuclear bomb on the organisation. But, as Friedrich Schiller, the German poet, so aptly observed, '*Against stupidity the very gods themselves contend in vain.*' Taking a deep breath and swallowing scathing criticism of my predecessor, I asked, '*Where do we start to rebuild confidence in Quality Management?*'

'*Operations. They had to suffer most in the aftermath of the dismantling of our Q-systems. – I know, it is the largest chunk but people there really crave for well-oiled processes.*' – '*Understood*' I said and added '*but we have to start with a smaller pilot project so we can show some success in a short period of time.*' – '*Then let's take shipping. They are always happy to have the goods they need to expedite on time in full,*' the CQO answered merrily.

'*Then that's where we start*', I said, adding, '*It's 5pm now. I want a preliminary-state value stream map of the procedures and processes concerning shipping on a large enough empty wall not later than 7 o'clock this evening. Dismissed.*'

With a mock but well-practised salute (learned during his former career as an army captain) and a jubilant '*Sir! Yes, sir!*', the CQO went to look for the head of shipping and a large enough empty wall. At ten to seven, I started to look for a once-empty wall and found it, along with a dozen people embroiled in eager discussion. They quietened down when I approached, and after polite introductions were made, I asked the CQO to brief me on what they had come up with. The value stream map looked like a knitting pattern from a women's magazine. With a tour guide as apt as the CQO, I got the gist of it quickly enough to be able to take part in the discussion. An hour later, we had agreed on what procedures and processes needed to be re-implemented by the departments further upstream and within the shipping department.

We scheduled a meeting with the other C-level managers for the next day to agree on the best way forward in revitalising the once functional Quality Management system. Thanks to the well-prepared Quality Management documents, we made short work of implementing the new measures. The department heads appointed by my predecessor and still in agreement with my predecessor's opinion on Quality Management, received an invitation into my office for a one-on-one crash course on this subject. In a scenario 3 environment, people slow on the uptake experience the severity of Darwin's law of survival of the fittest...

Why did I tell this story and what's the *kaikaku* effect?

Because even in a pigsty, you might find some long-forgotten and even longer-cast pearls. Not everyone can distinguish jewels from baubles, so make sure to keep your mind open and your eyes peeled for even the slightest shimmer in the dark. Unfortunately, fools always find other fools who agree with them that discrediting the keepers of law and order is a good idea. It's not – it's the worst idea ever: without order and discipline, you '*have a ghastly mess*', Mr Banks informed his children in the 1964 movie *Mary Poppins*.

Between anarchism and a sclerotic statism is enough room for balanced and harmonious regulations/freedom-of-action relationship. The right path between regulations and freedom of action is a very thin and highly volatile one. Thus, you should keep reviewing and renewing the rules and regulations in your Quality Management manual to prevent them from becoming sclerotic.

The *kaikaku* effect in this anecdote is one down. – The downside of radical change is the destruction of healthy company cultures. In the story above greed triggered a radical change in the leadership, which triggered the unshackling from the fetters of rules and regulations from quality management system, which allowed progress in leaps instead of steps. – Remember the results of Mao Zedong's *'The Great Leap Forward'*: 30 million Chinese died.

3.3. The CHRO (Chief Human Resources Officer) in scenario 3:

Together with the interim manager, the CHRO tries to entice key personnel to stay on board and ease the way off the sinking ship for non-essential employees who want to leave of their own free will. True to the adage *'Never let a good crisis go to waste'*, it is also the CHRO's duty to reshuffle and outplace employees who might be happier in different careers within or outside the company. The CHRO has to keep his eyes peeled for employees who master crisis situations better than their peers and who come up with creative solutions to tricky problems. *'Desperation can be as powerful an inspirer as genius,'* Benjamin Disraeli remarked. Even in the biggest crises, the CHRO must keep his eyes on the long-term future of the company and find the right employees to implement *monozukuri* (も の づ く り , Japanese for 'craftsmanship'), a sincere attitude to produce something with pride, innovation and perfection, because nothing excels more than excellence.

A motto for the CHRO:

'I invest in people, not in business plans' – Warren Buffet.

Why did I choose this particular quote? Because the CHRO has to live up to his name and be concerned with the human capital of the company. I do not know of any business plan within the manufacturing industry that can be achieved without people; people are always more important than business plans.

An anecdote about the CHRO in a scenario 3 environment:

Every rescue project is prone to fail if some members of the rescue team run around like headless chickens or are scared shitless to act. These people have to be replaced at once. Note that replaced does not necessarily mean sacked – they might do a great job in peacetime but be unable to muster up the nerves to do so when the going gets tough.

At a company, I had to navigate out of unchartered waters the COO was acting like a headless chicken and the CFO was scared shitless. To quote Napoleon (the pig in George Orwell's *Animal Farm*, not the other one), *'All animals are equal, but some animals are more equal than others'* – this applies to C-level managers as well. In a scenario 3 situation, the CFO could be 'more equal' than the CEO (or so I was told by a banker from a large German bank) because the CFO has to talk to creditors and assure them that they will get their money back, given time.

Thus, an anxious and frightened CFO will make the creditors nervous, and nervous creditors might do things they'll regret once they've calmed down. For a CRO, finance is an important issue, but it is not the only thing they have to take care of. Thus, I suffered dearly for having to allocate so much time to this particular department. Besides, I am not really the best person to sweet talk creditors into keeping their feet still (you'll see why when you read my anecdote about the CFO in a scenario 2 environment).

However, what has to be done must be done, so with a lot of effort and self-discipline, I managed to smooth nerves all round. The creditors agreed to cut us some slack by allowing us to tender in written, instead of in-person, reports. The big advantage of reporting in writing is that you do not have to prepare them yourself, just to peruse what has already been put together. This freed up some time in my tight-as-a-duck's-arse-in-choppy-weather schedule, so I was able to have a heart-to-heart with the CHRO. After about three hours of going through a list of the names of current and former employees with a fine-tooth comb, we managed to find replacements for the CFO and the COO.

The potential new COO had been working successfully in this department for the company a couple of years back but had been fired for insubordination by one of my predecessors (who had been keener on having people around him who would take care of the hygiene of his backside than those who would look out for the wellbeing of the company), and the new CFO was already working within the company but had been demoted by the same predecessor to a mere clerk in procurement. The anxious CFO was happy to vacate his position and take some time off by arranging a lengthy sick leave with his GP – I instructed the CHRO to engage an outplacement provider to help him find new professional challenges outside the company once he was fit for work again. The headless head of operations' (aka COO) employment contract was terminated, and he was released from his duties with immediate effect.

I always like to step in as COO if the opportunity arises – there is always some fun going on in the factory. The former COO – let's call him Mr X – who I had dug out with the help of the CHRO, was working for a competitor. It's always a tricky situation to get someone out of his employment contract; some people like to return to a company they had previously worked for, while others cannot imagine returning to work for a company that had sacked them. Mr X was somewhere in between: he was not all too keen to return but was not averse to the idea, either. I met him on neutral ground in a restaurant at a motorway filling station. Slightly amused about his taking over the lead of the interview, I gave way and dutifully answered all his questions. He took up responsibility as the new COO three months later, once his notice period had expired.

I had not witnessed such a quick and sustainable success than the one I saw with this man. He inspired not only his direct reports but also the other employees at the company with his enthusiasm for lean management and his 'Let's do it now!' Stop- and-fix the problem before you go on.' approach.

By the way, the competitor was not happy about losing Mr X, but as fate would have it, five years after he left that employer, he had to (involuntarily) return, because this very competitor (or at least the multinational group it belonged to) had become the major shareholder in a friendly (at least for some) takeover of the company he had returned to

Why did I tell this story and what's the *kaikaku* effect?

Because the CHRO has to keep a good record of unfairly dismissed employees and employees who left the company of their own free will but who left a gaping hole in the department, they had been working in. People like these are assets, and they might show great willingness in returning to the fold. Thus, try to get high performers back (almost) at any cost. This is particularly good advice in a scenario 3 situation, where each and every able pair of hands is needed to drag the cart out of the mud.

The *kaikaku* effect in this anecdote was an upside one because neither the COO nor his direct reports needed any time at all to get used to each other but could make things happen at once. - Recalling once, or even several times, sacked staff can turn out to be a double-edged sword, thus, act with circumspection when you intend to reinstate a 'has-been'.

3.4. The CFO (Chief Financial Officer) in scenario 3:

The CFO makes sure that accounting keeps all books up to date 24/7, because finance has to provide cash-flow charts for the management, banks and liquidator. The controlling department needs to keep the internal and external reports up to date 24/7 for pretty much the same reasons. Some interim managers like to have the latest figures at hand, but most rely on this phase entirely on their intuition, which shows them whether they are on the right track. However, some key performance indicators (KPIs) need to be monitored, compared to the baseline and displayed for everyone to see. People lose hope fast in a crisis and gain confidence out of even minuscule progress (hint: '*hope dies last*'). That is why you have to share even the tiniest of successes with your employees, stake- and shareholders.

A motto for the CFO:

'All great truths begin as blasphemies' – George Bernard Shaw.

Why did I choose this particular quote? Because each of the three mentioned departments usually has enough elbow room to make figures look nicer than they are. – Do not give in to temptation: just present your figures as accurately and as truthfully as possible. If you do, you will see why I chose this quote.

An anecdote about the CFO in a scenario 3 environment:

This is a story about accounting and the relativity of time. Banks are well known for their generosity in extending credit lines and loans when a company would view these as 'nice to have' but are even better renowned for their stinginess in doing so when the company sees them as 'must haves'. Bankers loathe the unforeseen, especially if it is detrimental to them. So, to imbue themselves in a (false) sense of security, they ask for best-case and worst-case scenario financial plans. – Bankers seem to be unaware of what Albert Einstein had to say about planning: *'planning replaces coincidence by error.'*

Excel, ever so patient, accepts all sorts of weird figures that tally up to what bankers want to see. In this instance, it so happened that we had to ramp up sales figures to get the cashflow and overall financial results that the bankers had stipulated as a condition for extending a vital credit line – never mind the hockey stick effect that these figures showed in Excel. However, the market and the expectations of the bankers did not match, so every month, we were short on sales and long on bankers' anxieties. The sales team, usually a cornucopia of excuses, ran out of them and just shrugged timidly (which is completely out of character, isn't it?) when asked what reasons we could give for yet again failing to meet the forecasted sales figures.

Strangely enough memories from my childhood pop up when I find myself in a crisis situation. Mainly these are memories of school, with its occasionally Dickensian teachers and dreary homework that in those days, was a real pain in the proverbial. But neither your parents' nor the taxpayers' money will have been spent in vain if you can recall parts of the syllabus – for example, Einstein's special theory of relativity, which says that time decelerates or accelerates depending on how fast you are moving relative to something else. Approaching the speed of light, astronauts in a spaceship age much more slowly than people on earth.

Well, we were certainly moving towards bankruptcy at the speed of light, so we had to decelerate time if we wanted a chance to meet the forecasted sales figures. I asked IT to stop the clocks on the accounting department's PCs and to restart it if and when they had booked enough invoices to meet the sales forecast given to the banks. Saucer-sized eyes from the CIO and the CFO looked at me incredulously, trying to figure out whether I was joking, on drugs or actually serious about such a haywire idea. I assured them that it was the latter.

In retrospect, all went well, and I have often wondered when I could do this again. But there was one incident when the whole scheme could have been blown sky high: one of the omnipresent financial auditors (read also the anecdote about the CFO in a scenario 2 environment), a bit of a ladies' man, had been looking over the shoulder of one of the good-looking female accountants to verify some figures he was scrutinising. There was not a snowball's chance in hell that he would miss the date on the screen: it showed December in the beginning of February.

The accountant turned in her swivel chair to face him, blocking his view of the screen, and asked with a winning smile how she could be of assistance to him. '*Well, what I would like to know about your figures we can discuss over a nice cup of coffee, if you can spare the time,*' he ventured. And our accountant could spare the time!

Naturally, just halting time and hoping for the best will not necessarily result in success, so the sales team's virtual and collective noses were put to the grindstone and their efforts monitored on a daily basis by myself and even by the majority shareholder of the company. Who, by the way, happened to be the best salesperson in the company and who volunteered to get back on the road to sell his products. – By end of April, I was able to ask IT to set the accounting team's computers to the correct time.

Why did I tell this story and what's the *kaikaku* effect?

I admit that it was an underhanded trick (of sorts) that could have upset the apple cart and the trust that bankers had put in us as a management team; had they gotten wise to our testing of Einstein's special relativity theory.

The credit lines would have been rescinded with immediate effect, resulting in the end of a company with a shade over 300 employees and their families. But because the fiddling with time was a success, I can say 'No risk, no fun.' I will not, and I do not, encourage anybody at any time to take measures like the one described above.

However, there are circumstances beyond your zone of influence that can bring the company you work for crashing down. If and when you evaluate the results of these circumstances as prone to error by human judgement, then by all means, take unconventional countermeasures – just make sure that everyone involved knows how to keep mum about them. By the way, years later I suggested this 'stop time' procedure to the CFO of a company I was working for as a consultant: he refused the notion point blank and shunned me for at least two weeks. Recently I heard that this company had gone into governance by the banks...

The *kaikaku* effect in this anecdote was definitely an upside one: the unconventional measure of halting time gave sales enough time to set-up and execute their new sales strategy – which was selling directly to the end-users instead of OEMs (Original Equipment Manufacturers).

3.5. The CIO (Chief Information Officer) in scenario 3:

Any disruption in IT systems, especially in the enterprise resource planning (ERP) system, can be lethal. This is because any delays in delivery, for whatever reason, can cause a standstill in vital cash flow. Therefore, IT has to provide a 24/7 maintenance service.

A motto for the CIO:

'Failure is simply the opportunity to begin again, this time more intelligently' – Henry Ford.

Why did I choose this particular quote? Because who hasn't heard the joke about the demo version and the real thing? – (If you haven't, google it; then you will understand the meaning of this quote.

An anecdote about the CIO in a scenario 3 environment:

Six weeks to replace an ERP system from scratch in a company with about 300 employees is an accomplishment worth mentioning. I arrived at this particular company when scenario 3 conditions were in full swing, so there was no time to fix computer programs and we had to try to make the best of what was available. This was more of an impediment than a help in daily business dealings: the database was a mess, and its users were insufficiently trained. A quick-fix workaround helped to keep the company afloat. The CIO's verdict on the existing ERP system was: *'Dump it and get a new one!'* I hardly ever make a final decision on matters without triangulating the problem – in other words, I need the opinion of three independent sources on the same problem to be able to reach a conclusion on the best way forward.

In this particular case, I received dozens of opinions, all saying the same thing: *'Robert, we fucked up bigtime with the implementation of the current ERP system five years ago. Data migration was a cock-up, too, and users were left to their own devices to figure out how to use the program.'* I asked the CIO to look for a new ERP system, present three to the management board and, in the meantime, clean up the database as much as possible.

The CIO put his seven-leagues boots on, and in no time, management had to decide which of the presented ERP systems to choose. Being under pressure in their respective departments, the managers chose the one that was easiest to use and had a vast array of add-on modules. In a kick-off meeting the CIO and the ERP provider were asked to get the ball rolling Asap and were then left to their own devices. Right after the decision about which ERP system to implement had been made, we ran into a nasty piece of weather with the company: within two weeks, the crisis had increased to a level where management was tempted to surrender and acknowledge defeat. Thus, everything but cashflow was put on the backburner.

I can concede that miracles do indeed happen; no one can remember how we got out of that specific crisis, but we did, and when the CIO noticed that management was receptive to issues other than cash flow, it announced, '*We are ready to take off with the new ERP system when you are.*' And they really were: from the kick-off meeting to the time when the last department confirmed they were operational with the new ERP system, only six weeks had elapsed.

Why did I tell this story and what's the *kaikaku* effect?

Sometimes things are so obvious to everyone involved that making a decision and setting the forces to fix the problem free is really a piece of cake. In this particular case, the CIO and his direct reports were really left entirely to their own devices: they did not have to forward progress reports, they did not have to bother with to-do lists, they were liberated from whatever regulatory restrictions existed within the company and they had the right to recruit whatever staff they need from other departments to clean up the master data base.

They used their freedom wisely. An ex-post audit on what management had consented to showed that we had made the right decision: it was the best deal that money could buy and the most versatile ERP program available on the market in those days. The CIO left the company soon after it got back on track after receiving the consent of management to set up his own shop. No one was surprised that he wanted to let his talent for organisation bear interest in his own enterprise.

Giving highly motivated employees enough elbow room is essential because without time-consuming progress reports to be given to management, they are left with more time to spend on solving the key problems. Letting excellent employees go might not sound like a bright idea, but based on my experience, it is an excellent idea because they will be extremely unhappy if they cannot walk the path they chose for themselves. Some high flyers may even return when they notice that starting an enterprise and being your own boss is not really a walk in the park. The CIO returned to the fold after two years of struggling as a freelancer, and his second career at the company was a win-win for both sides.

Letting go of good employees can be rather difficult in family-owned companies because the founder always perceives it as 'high treason' and the departing employee senses this – or may even be told as much in no uncertain terms. Returning to the fold, though, is usually no problem because the founder is convinced that his kingdom is better than any other.

The *kaikaku* effect in this anecdote is an upside one: Letting go of the reins and giving up supervision of direct reports and their essential projects is a rather tricky decision in a scenario 3 environment for any CEO/CRO. So much can go wrong and lead to irreparable disaster. – In the above case the CIO's approach to migrate only a minimum of data from the old ERP system to the new ERP system and to let clerks in each department key in the necessary data with each new customer order was the absolutely right one.

3.6. The CSO (Chief Sales Officer) in scenario 3:

Even though some readers will accuse me of cynicism, I say that usually, and unfortunately, not much changes for sales teams in a scenario 3 environment because they have been doing for years what they are officially asked to do now: sell as much as they can, as long as they do so with a positive contribution margin. It is, of course, not unheard of for a company on the brink of bankruptcy to have a substantially positive sales margin, but it happens, and some real squandering must have been going on at the company for a long, long time for it to be the case.

Mottos for the CSO:

'Egotism is the source and the summary of all faults and miseries' – Thomas Carlyle.

And, because the sales department is clearly my favourite, here is another one:

'Mistakes are the portals of discovery' – James Joyce.

Why did I choose these particular quotes? A significant percentage, if not the overwhelming majority, of the success of a company depends on the performance of the sales force: if they are egotistic (read: if they generate turnover without margin to cash in on their usually significant sales bonuses, for example), they will cause the same amount of harm as the percentage they represent. If they do not learn from their errors, the company's collapse is inevitable.

An anecdote about the CSO in a scenario 3 environment:

The people in sales work under similar stress as the people in finance preparing appropriate cashflow plans for creditors: if sales does not bring in business, there is no cash. If competitors learn about how tight a spot a sales team is in, they can easily outmanoeuvre them by giving larger discounts, shorter delivery times and overall better conditions to their mutual customers. That is why sales teams have to defuse all sorts of malicious rumours flying around in the market. They also need to exude a relaxed confidence with customers so as not to appear too keen to close the deal, even while they know that they cannot return from the hunt without a kill. This is no small feat if your own livelihood depends on it.

The CSO at a company I worked for as CRO knew all this and acted accordingly. He came up with a cock-and-bull story for his customers that general headquarters (GHQ), where the top dogs sit to rule over their subsidiaries, wanted to invest in new equipment if our subsidiary could just prove that market demand justified the capital expenditure. To his counterpart at our sister company he told a tall story about a sudden ramp-up in demand of the particular goods that our sister company could, but we could not, produce.

He and his sales team managed to get their order books well filled with such products, sold at a price level they announced as a 'once in a life time opportunity' for customers and under the condition that customers paid in advance for said goods. The aim of this kamikaze mission was to generate enough short-term cash for the company to get out of the woods.

The people in charge at GHQ and our colleagues at the sister company were not at all amused. Our orders had blocked their machine capacities, used their raw materials and put tension on the mutual cash pool because, to keep our subsidiary afloat, we diverted the money to other than the cash pool bank accounts. Readers with experience in these matters will know that measures such as these are last-ditch attempts to cling on – they out you as a pariah and paint your company as a rogue state in a shithole country, sadly. Sadly, because all we did was fighting for survival.

Why did I tell this story and what's the *kaikaku* effect?

I know it is below the belt to open bank accounts to divert money from the group cash pool. However, (even if any explanation of such business is futile, I will here attempt the impossible...) the subsidiary was on its very last legs. A takeover was imminent, and an increasing number of share- and stakeholders had joined the crowd shouting 'Divest!' at GHQ.

Before I put my reputation as an honest business man on the line, I tried to take up the big guys at GHQ on their high-flying vision, mission and commitment statements. I had always wondered whether these statements were just meant to look good on the website or whether they had been stated out of conviction.

It is not hard to guess that the top brass failed miserably: they refused any financial help point blank and decided the fate of well over 200 employees and their families with a Gallic shrug and a condescending *'We don't give a flying duck about your third-rate subsidiary Robert.'* – Then and there I decided on the above nefarious strategy to pull the subsidiary out by its own bootstraps.

Naturally, I received a third-degree dressing down by the CEO and CFO at GHQ for pulling this stunt. Legal actions against me were mentioned in anger but withdrawn instantly when I reminded them that failing to live up to their mission and vision statements could find its way to the media. – I gave them a piece of my mind about the importance of authenticity. They were not impressed but their rage assuaged – a bit – but let's just say that we do not send birthday or Christmas cards to each other.

A few months later, the group was sold to a financial investor who indulged in a 'make the bride pretty for the forthcoming marriage' capital expenditure. We got our special machine and could service our market with products that had a better margin. I never asked the new CEO at GHQ whether his predecessor had told him about the scam we had pulled off before the takeover, so I cannot claim with certainty that the former CEO kept it a secret due to my speech about values (or because it would have made him look like a real dupe that something like this could have happened right under his nose). I take vision and mission statements seriously and try to live up to them. Some are so farfetched that it is really hard to do so, but hey! – I am always on the look-out for a mission impossible!

The *kaikaku* effect in this anecdote is an ambivalent one: pulling wool over the eyes of your colleagues, sailing pretty close to the wind by diverting money from a cash-pool and causing a turmoil in the market with dumping prices might be a bit too much to rectify the rescue of a doomed subsidiary in a region with minor importance. – I leave it to the reader to decide whether such radical changes in loyalty are acceptable.

3.7. The CRDO (Chief Research & Development Officer) in scenario 3:

R&D departments need to provide a 24/7 service for procurement and operations because any materials, components, work-in-process goods, etc. found in a company's warehouse need to be assessed for whether they can substitute missing items in the bill of materials due to lack of cash or long delivery times. Operations, too, might have questions on how to assemble components, modules and such if they are doing so out of new materials. It is also a good time to fix any pesky bugs in the bill-of-materials list that operations and procurement have been asking about for years because late deliveries to customers due to missing parts could lead to insolvency or bankruptcy.

A motto for the CRDO:

'*Any sufficiently advanced technology is indistinguishable from magic*' – Arthur C. Clarke.

Why did I choose this particular quote? Because this is exactly what is expected of an R&D department: to create magical products that flabbergast and delight customers. Go for it!

An anecdote about the CRDO in a scenario 3 environment:

Research and development are long-term undertakings and are, therefore, hardly ever suitable for carrying out the quick fixes so desperately needed in times of crisis. R&D can bear its share of the burden by fostering adaptations, alterations and standardisations.

The company I worked for as an interim site manager had an OTIF delivery rate of around 40% when I was hired and was only still afloat because of hefty credit lines from the shareholding private equity (PE) firm. Customers were furious and were threatening punitive damages if on-time deliveries were not improved in the near future.

Almost all well-known consultancies (such as McKinsey, Boston Consulting Group, PriceWaterhouseCoopers and Bain) had run analysis and reported about the to-dos in the R&D department (and, of course, in all the other departments). Thus, as soon as the blue-chip consultancies had left the company, I only had to pick up where management had let go of the reins (a gross negligence from the PE side was not to include 'monitoring of the implementation progress' in the contract with the aforementioned consultancies – this was definitely penny wise but pound foolish). I asked the head of R&D to stop engineering and instead to implement the new design of front- and endplates they had on their virtual drawing board. This would reduce the variety of these parts tremendously, thereby simplifying procurement, warehousing and, in the long-run, after-sales services.

He went one step further and standardised the fastening bolts, systematising with his team the management of stamping tools in such a way that the handling time of tools could be significantly reduced. In the wake of the imminent crisis, R&D also standardised other parts.

Why did I tell this story and what's the _kaikaku_ effect?

In almost all departments and almost all companies, you can find employees who really care about the wellbeing of their employer and have plans, developments and concepts in their real or virtual drawers that they will present if given an opportunity to do so. Find these people asap; they are the nuts and bolts of _kaikaku_'s success. Experience shows that standardising the variety of goods that a sales team is allowed to sell during a scenario 3 situation gives a company a greater chance of post-crisis success. Standardised products have shorter lead times, so sales might opt to sell more of these to their customers – I know, I am an incurable optimist.

A word on blue-chip consultancies: as management or as interim manager, you can think of them what you want, but their analysis and reports are, in general, a big help because they contain a great deal of pre-crunched data. I doubt that any PE partner will ever read my book, but if one does, here is a piece of advice: always – really, in each of your projects – include 'monitoring of the implementation progress' in your contract with a consultancy firm. If you do not stipulate this in your contract, you will pay at least double, because the management of the company you have just bought will be reluctant to implement the suggestions of some just-graduated greenhorn from a big-name consultancy. It is even more unlikely that someone at McKinsey et al. will read this book, but if one does: you must have senior consultants in your employ who do not look freshly minted in academia and who insist on: implementation, implementation, implementation of the proposed measures!

The *kaikaku* effect in this anecdote is an upside one: It is not very common to turn a company in a scenario 3 situation around using the R&D department as a fulcrum. But alas! the department you start from is immaterial. What counts is: *'Give me a fulcrum and I'll move the world.'* - Archimedes

3.8. The CPO (Chief Procurement Officer) in scenario 3:

Procurement sets up a 24/7 service to get newly developed or amended materials and components as quickly as possible from existing and freshly acquired suppliers. Procurement is in a feedback loop with operations to assist in make-or-buy decisions based on production capacity and/or machine breakdowns.

A motto for the CPO:

'Adversity is the diamond dust Heaven polishes its most precious jewels with' – Thomas Carlyle.

Why did I choose this particular quote? Because procurement might be the department that faces the most adversity: under whatever conditions they close a business deal, it could have been better; of whatever quality the goods they purchase are, they could have been better, cheaper and faster delivered. From the vantage point of the suppliers, procurement is always too stingy, too demanding and entirely unrealistic about what can and cannot be done.

An anecdote about the CPO in a scenario 3 environment:

If the key role of the sales team in a crisis is to bring in cash, the key role of procurement is to drastically reduce cash outflow and look for suppliers with deep pockets and fast delivery times. In general, suppliers, especially at this stage, need to be very flexible and at their customers' beck and call.

A company I worked for operated with depleted cash reserves and could hardly make ends meet. Suppliers were about to set up camp at the company's premises to make sure that their invoices were paid. Indeed, the landlord of the factory's building ordered a security firm to block the entrances and exits to the premises until we forked out both the overdue rent and the rent to be paid in the next three months.

In such grave financial situations, suppliers often phone and threaten not only employees in accounting but also their contacts in procurement. To restore order in the procurement department, I set up a hotline for anxious suppliers to call and asked the head of procurement to man this hotline with his staunchest and most stress-resistant team members. All other phone numbers in procurement were replaced by new ones that were not communicated outside the company. Bar the employee handling the hotline, the procurement team could start looking for new suppliers that met the conditions set by the bank: that the headcount was drastically reduced, and that increased procurement volume was not allowed. Unfortunately, the bank had forgotten to provide us with some magic wands with which we could conjure up the products and services rendered by these now-redundant employees.

It was a typical catch-22 situation: if we stuck to the rules set by the bank, the company would soon turn belly-up because too much work would meet too few workers; if we kept to the headcount, the banks would cancel the credit lines. The head of procurement, a man with a healthy fighting spirit, went the extra mile and invested his out-of-office spare time to look for a supplier who was willing to take over part of an expensive production process within the company at his own costs – we were looking for a work-in-work contractor. It took the head of procurement some time to find the right partner for this gargantuan task, but eventually he did find one: the supplier not only bought the production machines from us but also employed our machine operators and auxiliary personnel so that we could show cash inflow (for the machines, raw materials and work-in-processes sold to the supplier) as well as a reduction in cash outflow (in terms of labour costs and raw materials' purchases) for the next six months because the head of procurement had also negotiated a grace period in which we did not have to pay for the services of the new supplier. To all the doubters out there: I know this had negative effects on the balance sheet, but it had a life-saving effect on cashflow. Let's repeat this: mantra: *'If cashflow is breathing and profit is food for a company, which can you survive longer without?'*

Why did I tell this story and what's the *kaikaku* effect?

The solution to your problems does not always have to come from you. It can also come from a supplier who is willing to take risks and has a long-term perspective. In this case it also took the determination of the CPO to go the extra mile to find such a supplier.

The *kaikaku* effect in this anecdote is an upside one: for a multinational corporation it is not unusual to have 'strangers' working in their factories. It is almost unheard of at mildly conservative, family-owned companies in Germany. Allowing non-employees to work on the premises, with equipment that formerly belonged to the company and not being able to order around former employees still sticking around on the premises is radical change indeed for a lot of patriarchs.

3.9. The COO (Chief Operating Officer) in a scenario 3:

The operations team produces only what is really needed, thereby disregarding 'optimal' production batches, set-up and change-over times, etc. and thus making the stipulations of preliminary costing, in general, ineffective. They finish the planned tasks every day, even if they have to work 24/7. Only finished goods can be billed and shipped. Together with Quality Management (and/or the health, safety and environment manager), they allocate enough time for occupational health and safety measures (see: 'OSHA'). In crisis situations, push comes to shove when accidents and sick leave increase. It might sound like madness to many but implementing lean management in the most critical area of operations will give you the best and shiniest lighthouse ever built as an advertisement of how successful lean management tools are. If you think this is impossible, remember how fast the Chinese built hospitals in the 2020 coronavirus crisis.

A motto for the COO:

'Quality means doing it right when no one is looking' – Henry Ford.

Why did I choose this particular quote? Because although operations really happen to be my favourite department (sorry, sales!), I know that they like to take shortcuts – to fix something they have botched up without accounting for it (see: 'ghost factory') – and that they generally like to do things their way, even if that way is not necessarily the best option.

An anecdote about the COO in a scenario 3 environment:

Time is essential, so everything that shortens lead time and accelerates deliveries results in earlier invoicing and faster cash inflow. An interim CRO is sometimes akin to a plumber fixing a bunged-up pipe: once the obstruction is cleared, the fluid gushes through the pipe unconcerned about its effect on, for example, a tap that has been left open. In the same way, it does not matter in what industry you find yourself in; you need more people to handle this sudden opportunity to decrease your backlog. The Germans have a saying for this: '*Viele Hände, schnelles Ende.*' which verbatim translates into '*Many hands, fast ends*' and has the same meaning as '*Many hands make light work*'. In well-developed and well-running economies, excess manpower is not readily available in the labour market, so quick fixes have to be found within a company.

Computer Numerical Control (CNC) machines, unmanned transportation systems and such as reduced labour intensity in the factory on the one hand and an inflated bureaucracy in paperwork on the other make the headcount of blue- and white-collar workers of many SMEs equal. It is particularly the case in the German family-owned ('Mittelstand') companies that a fair number of white-collar workers are previous blue-collar workers who have managed to get themselves a cushy desk job by merit or by irk (or is it jerk?).

These employees are worth their weight (usually increased due to their desk jobs) in gold because they can be redeployed to handle excess labour demand in factories. I used this approach regularly as a newly appointed general manager and kept up with this practice as an interim manager in many projects. I get mixed responses from the once blue-collar employees: some are happy to be back, but some dread the likelihood that they could get stuck in their old jobs again. The same applies to the people in charge, as some of the employees returning to their roots bring them cheers while others give jeers. Unfortunately, the sentiments of the two sides do not always match.

It was in final assembly where I needed extra pairs of hands for a task that only required knowing which way a screw has to be twisted to tighten it. In spite of the ease of the task, the pristine white-collar workers were put together with experienced blue-collar workers in a 24/7 week. After six weeks, we had managed to reduce the backlog not only on the one big order that the whole thing was set up for but also on other orders, because the white-collar workers liked the exercise so much that they asked their blue-collar colleagues to show them how more complicated products were assembled. In fact, the success was so overwhelming that some customers, who had received their orders not just on time but early, asked us to store the products because their incoming goods warehouses were overflowing. Another so-called side effect of this exercise was that a few weeks after the dust had settled and every employee was back at his own job, a young machine operator asked me on one of my regular tours through the factory whether I would agree to the opposite flow of workers. I must have looked dumbfounded, because he said, '*In plain English: the people from the office worked in the workshop. Can I – and any of my mates here – work in the office?*'

I frowned and said, '*Generally speaking, yes. But what would you want to do?*'

'*I would like to become a member of the Quality Management department.*' Always keen on getting someone from the workshop into Quality Management, I instantly agreed; he became one of the best auditors I have ever seen.

Why did I tell this story and what's the *kaikaku* effect?

Time is the maker and breaker of success in a scenario 3 environment. The more you can reduce its waste, the higher your chances to succeed at navigating the company back into chartered waters. Thus, use timesavers excessively and without (much) regard for individual sentiments. A crisis situation is much like a war: you are not necessarily fighting other people, but overbearing odds. It is mainly up to HR, though a non-partisan interim manager can be of much assistance, to decide which former blue-collar workers can return to their desks and which can be of more value when they remain in the workshop. The employees themselves might have different views for their best way forward, but experience shows that after their egos calm down, the vast majority of them are happy to be back in their old jobs. Job rotation is a technique far too underused in industrial companies. Use it extensively, even in, or maybe especially in, difficult situations.

The *kaikaku* effect in this anecdote was an upside and a downside one: the upside part is obvious. The downside is less so. I mentioned the workers' council (WoC; without the 'o' the abbreviation has a slight tendency to mislead) and its might in German companies throughout this book. The WoC is not keen on changes bar those favouring employees. Thus, asking them to give a hand in matters in a time of emergency triggers the question *'what's in it for us?'* – The honest answer to this often-asked question is *'you save your jobs.'* – Which is met with a snigger and an *'Oh come off it! Who do you think you can fool?! – The shareholders will never allow the company to go bust.'* – There is indeed truth in this and that is why the employer gives in to the outrages demands of the WoC. – In the above case we had to give in to some long time demands (like allowing employees to change from street to work clothes on the company's time – comptroller from GHQ told me that this amounts to €500k p.a.) to have the consent of the WoC to redeploy employees where they were needed most.

Chapter 4

There are no hard borders between scenario 3 and scenario 2 environments. It is more like a relay race, where the baton is handed over from the previous runner to the next one when both are at full speed. Once the interim manager thinks that it is the appropriate time to hand powers back to the CEO and/or management team, he will do so. In the meantime, a scenario 3 environment looks very much like a strong monarchy. Scenario 2 environments are where the aristocracy (i.e. the management) gets a say in matters once more.

Departments and their duties during *kaikaku* in scenario 2

4.1. The CEO in a scenario 2:

The CEO and the interim manager agree on a modus operandi for the duration of the project, which can have different phases. For example, the CEO hands over power to the interim manager for the difficult parts of the radical change procedures, but after these have been accomplished, they share competencies. When close to reaching scenario 1, the CEO should ask the interim manager to step into the background and to coach him. This approach enhances sustainability, provided that the CEO does it out of his free will and not because he is told to do so by the shareholders/liquidator. – A generous portion of humble pie is certainly a diet well recommended for CEOs.

An anecdote about the CEO in a scenario 2 environment:

When things are not running smoothly, each generation of a family-owned company will be convinced that the previous generation is to blame for a major oversight and that the next generation will never be fit to take the reins. These clear-cut borders get somewhat blurred when the seventh generation sits in the driver's seat and a strong father–child bond prevents 20/20 vision. In this case, even the most loyal CEOs and CFOs cannot make the chairperson see any reason why the business set up by the patriarch needs to be changed or even divested. Stooping to accounts, cost allocation and general profit fiddling are usually the last resorts before an interim manager is engaged and sent on the mission impossible of shutting down the legacy of a revered ancestor.

Desperation can lead to such a tactic, but if the power of lean management is unbeknownst to the instigators, such an approach can also backfire. Especially if the department in question has been treated like an unloved stepchild for the past twenty years. Dumping unwanted but un-sackable employees into one department for years is a sure way to have that department stick out like a sore thumb. Not all of these employees will deserve their fall from grace, however.

So, when I was assigned the task of 'saving department by getting rid of it' (the words of a CEO when he bade me goodbye after a plant tour of under ten minutes), the department was merrily ticking over on a low performance level. After the CEO had left, I stood for about an hour on an elevated balcony in front of the plant manager's office and observed the operations down below in the workshop. Eventually, the plant manager joined me and, to my relief, did just the same thing: he observed.

'Shall we go for a smoke?' I asked after a long enough period of time had elapsed for him to grasp the situation of the people under his care. After a very unhealthy dose of nicotine, we reached a mutual agreement on what needed to be done to lick the department into shape: we cut production space by half, eliminating vast amounts of work-in-process material by introducing one-piece flow, and replaced production-on-stock with a make-to-order system with immediate effect.

The changes took two months to implement, but once the financial figures of the third month had been taken into account, we received a phone call from the CFO inquiring, 'What the hell is happening out there?! The figures don't make any sense: stock levels are down, work-in-process is down, overtime is down, there are no part-timers anymore, but deliveries are up and OTIF jumped to well over 80%!' After the figures of the fourth month were out, the CFO visited the department – rumour had it that he had not done so for at least 10 years. To the utter surprise and delight of the 'untouchables', the well-liked chairperson had accompanied the CFO; he shook hands all around and even gave some hugs.

Why did I tell this story and what's the *kaikaku* effect?

During my tenure as CEO, I always obeyed one of my core beliefs that the responsibilities/duties of a top manager weigh more than the perks. Thus, my very good advice to all top managers is this: make doubly sure and think twice before you decide to divest a business unit, a subsidiary or even a company. Every divestment destroys values, destroys jobs and may lead to desperation and personal tragedies.

I always remind myself of a particular one of these personal tragedies so that I do not forget the seriousness of decisions to make people redundant. I once had to fire a good dozen employees to cut costs. I did so without much regard for personal hardships, basing it instead entirely on high cost and low performance criteria. Suffice it to say that one employee fell into such a deep psychological hole after he lost his job that he had to be admitted to a psychiatric clinic for a considerable period of time.

Therefore, only if and when each and every measure has been applied to a particular problem and all efforts have led to naught should business units be divested, people made redundant or, generally, values destroyed. This should not be mistaken for procrastination on vital decisions, however. A business unit bleeding red ink has to be propped up by profitable ones, but these subsidies are only justifiable when there is a fair chance of getting the sub-par unit back on its feet. If there is no chance of rescuing the unit, it has to be divested without delay; any postponement is unfair on the other business units since the money that profitable units generate could otherwise be invested in their own futures. In short, do not throw good money after bad!

The *kaikaku* effect in this anecdote is an 'all thumbs up': It shows in how short a period of time success can be achieved if there is no counterforce to the implementation of the changes. –

The 'untouchables' had nothing to lose because they could not slide lower in the food chain. They already bottomed out. – Thus, they did not mind to try an entirely different approach. – I never experienced the ideal situation where people enthusiastically participate in the implementation of the changes, thus, no headwind is good enough for me.

4.2. The CQO in a scenario 2:

CQOs should divide their time between assisting the interim manager and auditing newly created procedures and work instructions that make sure that everyone understands the new way of doing things. As scenario 2 gets closer to scenario 1, the quality managers should intensify training of the new procedures.

An anecdote about the CQO in a scenario 2 environment:

We were rollercoasting from scenario 2 into scenario 3 in a dizzying way. At board meetings, the chairperson cracked jokes such as *'Robert, we should only invite you to every even-numbered board meeting because then the company you are in charge of would always be even'*, or *'Robert, I am so totally with you. Doing the – pardon my French – fucking Mexican wave is awesome... when it's done at a stadium by several thousand gone-crazy-as-a-monkey's-arse fans, but not, I repeat not, by a fucking company!'* or – and this one was the final straw – *'Robert, we all envy you. You have the best work-life balance of any of us here because you managed to relocate your company to Bondi Beach, but mate – riding the waves might be fun for you, but trust me, it's no fun for us seeing your figures bobbing like tits at a stag do. Make it stop.'* I managed to make it stop – with the help of the CQO.

I had always been a big fan of Quality Management (even if I get drowsy when I have to read procedure and work instructions), and until that very day, I truly believed that I had made good use of it already. I was wrong. The potentials of Quality Management are unimaginable. While my fellow managing directors slept peacefully in their hotel beds before returning, well rested, to their factories the next day, I began my journey back to my factory right after the board meeting was adjourned. My guardian angel must have been on duty during my drive from the board meeting's venue back to the factory: despite my efforts to the contrary, I did not get any speeding tickets.

The factory was empty when I arrived in the small hours, so I strolled aimlessly around the machines, took a look at the dispatch area, ambled through the warehouse and was retracing my steps through the factory to go upstairs and head towards my office when a voice startled me: *'Have you fallen out of bed, Robert?'* The CQO addressed me as he stood in the unlit corridor. I let him in on the latest joke of our dear leader. He grinned and said, *'I thought you might return in a dark mood. That's why I am here so early. I want to check on the latest audit reports. Would you like to join me? My percolator is already on.'* Freshly brewed coffee is irresistible, so I gladly accepted. We drank gallons of coffee and talked until the place became busy around us. As soon as all heads of departments and their deputies were available for a quick meeting, we briefed them on what we had cooked up in the small hours:

'From this day on, all procedures and processes as stipulated in the Quality Management manual have to be audited on a daily basis. You are hereby all relieved from your operational day-to-day obligations for 10 days. Please cancel all your appointments, meetings and such, and start auditing your respective departments. After these 10 days, the deputies – who will be in charge of your departments while you are auditing – will take over for another 10 days. Should your direct reports still have difficulty following the procedures, we will start again, with another 10 days of audits by the heads of department followed by 10 days of audits by the deputies; we will repeat this as often as necessary.'

After the first 20 days of audits, the company worked like the proverbial Swiss cuckoo clock (proverbial, contrary to factual, because it was invented by one Franz Anton Ketterer in the Black Forest, which is actually in southern Germany). Finally, I stopped being the target of third-rate jokes by the chairperson because the figures of our company were even – even in odd-numbered board meetings.

Why did I tell this story and what's the *kaikaku* effect?

A gentle approach to encouraging employees to embrace change does not work all the time. In fact, it rarely does. On these rare occasions, for whatever reason, everyone and everything seems to fall into line automatically, and soon, the figures just seem to improve by themselves. However, this is the exception, not the rule. Sometimes, only laying down the laws and throwing the book at every culprit for the slightest mistake with a zero-tolerance policy is the only feasible strategy. This approach only works if the vast majority of the management (more than two out of three members) agree with it. In Germany, you also need in-writing consent from the workers' council. If your management team does not support such a radical method, stop it before you even start, because you will fail, not just losing face but also losing people's belief in you as a leader. However, if your management team agrees wholeheartedly with you on such harsh actions, do not shy away from them. Tighten the thumbscrews when everything else has failed. When travelling on this path, taking prisoners is a no-no, as is looking any other way than forward...

The *kaikaku* effect in this anecdote was an upside one in the long run and a downside one in the short run: Financial figures took a nose dive during the audit process and a significant number of employees were not amused at all to be treated like kindergarten children. A lot of effort and energy went into explanations and discussions. Once we got them on our side of the track success was inevitable.

4.3. The CHRO in a scenario 2:

Whether arriving directly at scenario 2 or getting there via scenario 3, The CHRO's main duty at this stage is to push the reshuffling and outplacement process and start looking for training and coaching courses for the remaining employees. After living through scenario 3, people usually do not want to repeat these experiences. They will do whatever it takes to prevent such a situation from reoccurring. The CHRO must use this employee euphoria to acquire new, hopefully habit-changing knowledge to its fullest extent.

An anecdote about the CHRO in a scenario 2 environment:

A scenario 3 environment is like a battlefield on which you are fighting for the survival of your troops: there is not much time to think about what the future will hold once the fighting has ceased. Embroiled in a war-room-like atmosphere with your management team, it is not always easy to detect when you have crossed the imaginary line from scenario 3 into scenario 2, so a tap on the shoulder from someone less entangled is always welcome. In this story, it was an HR head who made me see that the worst was over by asking,

'Is it okay if we have in-house Quality Management courses in the next three months, followed by three months of in-house training in lean management basics?' It took me a while to get the meaning of what he had just said because I was thinking, *'What the...?! We are here in the middle of a bloody war and this bloke wants to send combat soldiers to training courses?!'*

Until I had gathered my wits (a remark from a former supervisor in my younger years shot through my mind: *'Robert, we cannot push the company into a crisis just to make you feel good'*), the CHRO went on, saying,

'We are all grateful to you for leading us through these most difficult times in the history of our company, and we all appreciate your fighting spirit, but most of us would like to leave battle stations and return to our civilian lives, if you don't mind.'

'Indeed', I said. *'I must have got carried away by all these actions we initiated. However, as you know, it is not speed that kills you, but a sudden stop, so I will decelerate proceedings slowly so that you can start with the training courses in six weeks, okay?'*

'Agreed,' he said, adding, *'I thought you were going to say something like that. The first in-house Quality Management training course starts in two months' time.'*

Why did I tell this story and what's the *kaikaku* effect?

It is very easy to get carried away when you find yourself in the eye of a storm, so any signal that the worst is over should be welcomed. Generally, heads of departments who have managed to lead their teams out of the woods are well advised to restore anything resembling normality carefully: it really is the sudden stop that kills, so pressure should be released step by step. Deploy any employees still in a fighting mood to departments that are still in dire straits. Departments operating on a reduced stress level can be of more assistance to those still involved in restructuring their internal processes. Success is always an accumulation of the efforts of a multitude of participants. Regardless of your involvement in the good fight, try to get an overview of the whole situation as often as possible, and if you cannot, listen to those who have a better grasp of the status quo than you. For an interim manager, leaving one battlefield for another one around the corner is not unusual – but remember, not everyone likes to spend their days fighting.

The *kaikaku* effect in in this anecdote is a debatable on: With some justification you can ask '*What was the radical change part here Robert?*' – It is almost entirely an idiosyncratic one: I absolutely detest, loath and hate to be stopped when I am on the move to change things for the better. The CHRO was 'cruising for a bruising' by suggesting training courses for key employees in the middle of a bloody battle. – I might not be the only old warhorse hard to stop when charging.

4.4. The CFO in a scenario 2:

The crisis for the CFO is only over when the creditors, and above all, the banks, are satisfied and the liquidator has left the company for good, so continue doing what was done in scenario 3 until then.

An anecdote about the CFO in a scenario 2 environment:

Here is a story about chartered public accountants from the 'Big Four' (Deloitte, Ernst & Young, KPMG and PwC), called *'Eine Lüge ist gestattet um der Wahrheit zum Siege zu verhelfen'* (*'a lie is permitted to help truth to triumph'*) – Anonymous. The company I worked for was in dire straits, so the creditors had appointed a chartered public accountant to audit the company every week. Actually, one or two junior auditors were present almost every single day. Needless to say, they ran out of sensible work after a while and started to inspect the company's inventories. After several weeks of meticulous work, they came up with the verdict:

25% to 30% of the inventory had to be depreciated.

This would result in the liabilities exceeding the assets, and the overextension would force the CEO to commence bankruptcy proceedings. Never missing an opportunity to pick up deliberately or accidently dropped gauntlets in those days, I summoned the auditors' supervisor and asked him how his henchmen had come up with such scandalous figures.

'Henchmen? Well, really, Mr Carter, you don't mince your words, do you? – They took random samples,' he said.

'Random samples?!' I asked incredulously.

'Yes, random samples,' he said. Just to make sure there was no misunderstanding (and to give the head honcho of one of the Big Four the opportunity to lie to me again), I asked the CFO and one of the omnipresent junior auditors to join us in the meeting room and asked again how the outrageous figures of 25% to 30% had popped up.

'Random sampling,' said Jezebel, the junior auditor, looking sheepishly at his supervisor. I made her repeat the answer three times, including the number of samples (107), before letting the CFO and the junior auditor leave the room.

'We need time to forge a contingency plan,' I demanded.

'*You know as well as I do that no contingency plan will help you to get out of this,*' the supervisor of the auditors said acidly.

'*Nevertheless, we need at least a month to get this straightened out,*' I said, more forcefully than I had intended to.

'*Two weeks,*' he said as he lifted his oversized behind from the chair and left the meeting room. I did not want to lose any time getting into gear, so I immediately asked the CPO and my assistant to join me in my office. I asked the CPO to print a list of all items on stock, take a very good look at it and memorise the items with fast turnover rates and some of the items with slow turnover rates. I asked my assistant to get an appointment at a notary as soon as possible. A couple of days later, the CPO randomly chose 107 samples out of the list of items on stock, witnessed, signed and stamped by a notary.

The chartered public auditor turned up like a bad penny exactly at the end of the two-week deadline. With mock sympathy, he apologised for the procedures he would have to set in motion that would, very unfortunately, result in the bankruptcy of the company.

'*Not so fast!*' I chipped in before reminding him of his answer about how the samples were taken.

'*How could I forget?*' He sighed for effect. '*No one has asked me the same question as many times as you did.*' Once this issue was settled, I produced the random sampling report, signed by the notary, and announced that according to this *real* random sample, taking the inventory depreciation rate on dead stock would be a mere 0.6%. Never in my life before or since have I witnessed someone more baffled, taken aback, even gobsmacked than this man. The cocksure attitude went down the drain and took loftiness and condescension with it.

Slowly, it dawned on him what this meant, and when the penny eventually dropped, his shoulders sagged and he started to shake his head in slow motion, mumbling something incoherent. Dealing the deathblow to his intention to make us shut up shop, I said,

'*Naturally, I am prepared to have your random sampling and our random sampling contested in a court of law.*'

Having shaken off the shock of the epiphany, he said, '*That will not be necessary. I know when I am beaten. We have to agree, though, on a mutually acceptable depreciation rate on the dead stock.*'

'*Sure,*' I said. '*We'll do 4% on dead stock older than two years, 2% on dead stock older than a year. That is my first and final offer.*' Looking at me with almost pitiable doom in his eyes, he nodded in the affirmative. Before he could entirely regain his senses, I asked him to tell his henchmen about our agreement. He nodded again. Thus, I asked his colleague and my CFO to join us in the meeting room. Stone-faced, he told the junior auditor about the 4% and 2% depreciation agreement. Jezebel's mouth opened and shut several times, but no sound made it through her dry throat.

The CFO put his paw on the junior auditor's shoulder and said good-naturedly, '*Let's get to it! We have to report the latest figures to the banks in only three days and there is still a lot to do.*' They left, while I stayed in the room with the chartered accountant, who looked at me and said, '*I hope you make good use of the time you've gained with your little ruse.*' After a pause, he added, '*And I hope that you succeed in saving the company.*' With that, he said goodbye, and we have not seen each other again since.

Why did I tell this story and what's the *kaikaku* effect?

Yes, we did cheat in the valuation of the inventory and we were caught red-handed, with our pants down and on the wrong foot by the chartered accountant. The cruel, sheer truth that 'game over' was inevitable made me come up with such an unexpected and unconventional move. There was nothing to lose and all to be gained. – I am sure only sheer desperation can make you receptive for ingenious solutions to unsolvable problems. – The message here is: '*It is only over when the fat lady stops singing, and she never does, because your tinnitus sounds just like her.*'

The *kaikaku* effect in this anecdote is a non-debatable one: Without this radical change in attitudes towards the findings of the chartered accountant the company would have gone into bankruptcy procedures. – There are times and situations where you are at a real 'point of no return' and a 'point of unalterable decision': take the wrong decision and be doomed.

4.5. The CIO in a scenario 2:

Much like the CFO, the CIO has to uphold a 24/7 service until the crisis is over. As scenario 1 gets closer, IT should intensify the debugging and cleaning of master databases and draw up a priority list of what IT systems should be replaced, based on the experiences gathered during scenario 3.

An anecdote about the CIO in a scenario 2 environment:

IT plays a major role in making *kaikaku* happen (just read my anecdote about the CIO in a scenario 1 environment), and this is especially so in our digitalised world. Usually, databases are in sorry shape, with multiple entries and often prehistoric or false data cluttering the ERP and other vital programs. Fixing databases can take a long time, which the company does not have at this stage.

Reliable data is especially crucial in this scenario for a variety of reasons, including financial and KPI progress reports to the creditors and other stakeholders, machine performance data for operations, and production-routing algorithms. Under regular circumstances, ERP workarounds must not be encouraged, but in a crisis situation, (almost) everything is allowed.

Once, a company with an on-time-in-full (OTIF) delivery of well under 50% hired me to improve this KPI as quickly as possible. The OTIF delivery measure is a result of various processes in different departments, so to improve OTIF delivery, a number of processes have to be fixed first. At this company, the production planning was below par, or rather the Gantt program that they were using was not up to the task because it was far too cumbersome to use. It took the production planning team a long time to key in all the required data to introduce an additional machine into the production routing chain.

Only the most versatile machines were connected in the ERP system, leaving older, less versatile machines idle. Idle machines in a manufacturing company with a hefty customer order backlog are absolute no-nos. Thus, we needed a quick fix while the production planning team worked on a long-term solution. I told a young programmer in the IT department what I wanted: each and every machine in the company, not just the versatile machines that could perform multiple operations, had to work on orders. These versatile machines had a capacity overload of 300% to 400%. I also wanted real-time information about the production progress of the manufacturing orders.

He scratched his head and said, '*Well, if that's all you need and you can live without the bells and whistles, I can have it ready in two weeks.*'

'*Sorry mate, but that's too late,*' I said in a tone of voice that I know people do not argue with. I added, '*All I need is to know whether order number 4711 has been processed at machine A, yes or no, if it has arrived at machine B and so on, and finally whether it has arrived at the warehouse and whether it has been booked.*'

His eyes lit up. '*Okay, now I am getting your drift! You do not need to know when the order was started or how long it took to process it; you only want to see flags popping up on its way through the factory, right?*'

'*You're bang on, mate. That's all I need.*' I got what I wanted within 24 hours.

Why did I tell this story and what's the *kaikaku* effect?

Think very hard about the absolute minimum amount of information you require to make a decision or to be able to inform someone else who needs that information to carry on with his process. Then ask IT to write an algorithm and to implement it asap. Yes, usually you do not get any statistics out of such a highly simplified system, and you have to do a lot of manual handling –

like in the anecdote above where we had to shift the overcapacity from the versatile machines to the single operation ones without a routeing order – but ask yourself: do you really need historical data at this stage, or is it enough to know that the ball is rolling? Make sure that the workaround is temporary – just like a catheter is when a patient is in intensive care. You do not want to be caught dead with a catheter inside you outside a hospital, right?

The *kaikaku* effect in this anecdote was an upside one: It show how fast you can progress if you really just take the 'must-haves' with you and leave the 'nice-to-haves' behind.

4.6. The CSO in a scenario 2:

During scenarios 2 and 3, the CSO and his department managed to acquire multiple new customers due to the low sales margins authorized by the CEO. These new customers should be evaluated and categorised so that they can be served according to each category's needs.

An anecdote about the CSO in a scenario 2 environment:

The sales department should be left to their own devices to perform well. They need to be unshackled from regulations, unconstrained by small-minded comptrollers, and unobstructed by lead time. They would like to be totally uncommitted. However, a free reeling salesforce results in a pompous, complacent, and chaotic sales organisation that practices shotgun vending where they shoot at everything that moves and hope to hit something big. Often, such a sales strategy results in misery because the R&D department has to deviate from standards or design, being new and untested. The procurement department might not be able to obtain the correct products timely or in the correct quality and required quantity.

The operations department might have to manufacture and assemble something they have never done before, while finance might not agree with the agreed-on payment terms. For every department, excluding sales (based on their demands for freedom of action) standard procedures should be the objective. The £1 million question is whether the sales process should be standardised. Although it can, sales departments do not like the idea since the standardisation process resembles the saddle in an exceptionally vicious horse breaking. (To understand this metaphor, watch DreamWorks Picture's 'Spirit', especially the scene where the commanding officer of the fort tries to ride the horse after he had been left without water and food for a considerable period of time).

Standardising sales was not my idea and I was enormously sceptical as to whether it could be achieved.

My *sympathies* for pompous, complacent, and overbearing salespeople helped me to stomach the severe measures and endless hours that needed to be taken to get the sales department within the boundaries we wanted them in. The concept was simple enough:

Cluster customers according to their preferences along with their paying and buying habits and allocate matching salespeople to each cluster.

There was no one in the company who believed that it could be done and that it would work. Neither did I, but as CEO I had to believe in and promote this approach whole-heartedly, which I did because of my deep-felt *love* for sales.

The sceptics were proven wrong: sales margins improved, customers satisfaction increased, and we got a bigger slice of the market share. In addition, almost all the salespeople were, after a few months, happy to work the clusters that they had been assigned to.

Why did I tell this story and what's the *kaikaku* effect?

Not all great ideas necessarily have to be your own. You can either steal with pride (encouraged by 'yokoten'(横展 , Japanese for horizontal deployment or, loosely, copy and improve), from your sister companies within the group or, as a last resort, execute orders from GHQ.

Doesn't the exception prove the rule? – I love the part in the 1970s movie 'Patton' where he receives a direct order from Eisenhower and tells the soldier who operates the wireless to send back *'message garbled stop proceed as I think best stop'* or something to that account.

I must admit that there are times when GHQ gets it right, albeit rarely, but when they do, their orders should be put into action immediately. Clustering/standardising sales in a scenario 2 environment is not ideal, but you cannot expect GHQ to get everything right. They either get the to-dos right but the timing wrong, or they get the timing right but the to-dos wrong. Be lenient: taking decisions from an ivory-tower perspective is not easy and no situation, regardless of the severity thereof, justifies a descent to the 'little people'.

The important parts of standardising the sales department are:

1) take enough time to define the clusters (not more than six, otherwise you might end up with a cluster for every single customer, which is what the sales department would strive for);
2) leave yourself enough time to allocate customers into the best fitting clusters;
3) rather swap or fire and rehire salespeople than allocate non-matching ones to the clusters.

If you have done everything right after two–three months, the sales department will let you know that they had wanted to work this way all along, but were not allowed to.

The *kaikaku* effect in this anecdote is an upside one although it was triggered by GHQ: Restructuring and reorganising any department radically is always tricky because processes and functions get destroyed. The sales department is more equal than the other departments because if this department does not perform the other departments cannot perform. No matter how well they are organised and structured. – Clustering is akin to standardisation and therefore a success in and by itself. – Salespeople, in general, are not all too hard to reform because they strive on success. – If you can give them the means to get more and better orders, they will shed the old ways like a snake sheds its skin.

4.7. The CRDO in a scenario 2:

Using the momentum created by scenario 3 in redesign and streamlining, The CRDO starts with standardising raw materials, parts, and finished goods. A lack of self-discipline in sales teams is their second nature, which management must learn to cope with. A lack of self-discipline in R&D teams is not unheard of but when it prevails, disaster looms. Thus, the walls of every R&D office should state, in capital letters: STANDARDISE, STANDARDISE, STANDARDISE.

An anecdote about the CRDO in a scenario 2 environment:

We already saw the light at the end of the tunnel (and it wasn't an approaching train), being the end of scenario 3, when we came up with the idea of an industrial franchise system. In those days, franchise stood for 'McDonald's' and enthusiasm for this notion was very low. Meeting product safety requirements in a company's country of origin was difficult enough, but having to meet such requirements in international markets was an entirely different matter, particularly if it was an SME, rather than a multinational, stock-exchange-listed company required to meet such demands.

The CRDO wanted to know the countries we intended to start looking for franchise partners. He took careful notes and promised to come back asap with the results of his desk research. According to the information he was able to gather, the situation was much rosier than we all had thought, thus, we set sail to new shores. We soon learned that each franchise partner had different needs and desires, which soon led to a 'work overflow' in the R&D department.

Keen to help, the CRDO suggested training the engineers of the new franchise partners in our company and at the site of the franchise partner. He arrived prepared with a feasibility and training plan and we rubber stamped it at the board meeting so that training courses for engineers from various countries could commence. Our engineers soon enough learned that teaching others also meant learning from others. Many good and even great ideas were borne during these courses. Even if the engineers could not understand each other verbally, they always understood each other when paper and pencils were available to express themselves in hand sketches. Our engineers visited the sites of the franchise partners and learnt valuable insights and ideas about manufacturing processes and design studies, among others. All this new information could only be handled with a standardised CAD programme that produced standardised technical drawings and bills of material in a consistent language (English). If R&D or management allowed the franchise partners to set up their own CAD systems, a lot of time would have been wasted converting data from different systems. Imagine the possibilities with 20 or 30 franchise partners that could exchange data with each other.

If the reader misses the 'standardisation of products' in this context I have to mention that the product we sold had to be assembled with standardised modules. The alterations needed for the modules to be fit for worldwide distribution were marginal.

Why did I tell this story and what's the *kaikaku* effect?

R&D cannot always come up with something revolutionary; it must also be able to adapt existing products to different market needs and regulations. R&D is not only about engineering, but also about training, explaining, and co-operation with other internal and external departments, as well as encompassing STANDARDISATION.

After two years, our industrial franchise system became so famous that we did not have to actively look for new franchisees because they were looking for us. One of the funniest stories with a potential franchisee was regarding a Russian product design. A Russian company approached us with the notion of getting our brand name on their product. We were justifiably sceptical since the design showed idiosyncratic Russian sturdiness. The design had no chance of getting our brand name, like the prospect of sticking the 'Ferrari' brand on a 'Moskvich'.

We received a lot of product design ideas from a variety of countries. These posed always a challenge to our R&D department because they were used to develop a new product from scratch and had no experience in adapting those foreign product designs to make them look like they had been designed by us.

The *kaikaku* effect in this anecdote is a minor one on R&D: Actually, the idea to sell our industrial products in a franchise system was radically new. – Family-owned SMEs are not really keen on sharing their know-how with third parties. They rather stretch their financial limits to breaking point by establishing subsidiaries country by country than to co-operate with existing companies in those countries. Although this company had a couple of licence agreements running the shareholders showed remarkable reluctance to take licensing a step further to a basic franchise system where the franchisee had to pay an entrance fee to be allowed to produce and market existing products and a royalty to be able to participate in newly developed products and products adapted to the franchisee's market.

4.8. The CPO in a scenario 2:

Like the CSO with new customers, the CPO was required to acquire new suppliers to make ends meet during scenario 3 and cluster suppliers. Clustering suppliers in the same way as customers [see 'An anecdote on the CSO in a scenario 2 environment'] made sense because

1) the same system was used;
2) the same benefits, like job satisfaction, would be obtained; and
3) keeping your suppliers happy is as important as keeping your customers happy because they are part of the same value stream.

An anecdote about the CPO in a scenario 2 environment:

I would have never believed that as an economist cum MBA I would get death threats. My wife and two underaged sons (not even in their teens) had to host two policewomen for 48 hours as a measure of protection because a supplier threatened to abduct my sons. Unlike me, the board of directors was more shocked and concerned about the death threats by a venal supplier, who had paid backhanders to the CPO to stay listed. The board of directors' decision was, for once, unanimous and immediate: the rogue supplier needed to be sued in a court of law and business operations had to cease immediately. These measures, however justifiable under the given circumstances, caused disruptions in production and delays in shipments. The company was on its way back to a scenario 3 environment, which I could not allow.

I asked the new CPO (the old one's contract had been terminated with immediate effect; after learning what his paymaster was capable of and being shocked, he admitted to the backhanders) to circumnavigate the board's decision to cease business relations with the supplier and try to at least get the finished goods from their warehouse shipped to us asap. '*Well,*' he said, '*as soon as I heard what this filth did to you and your family, I took instant action by getting the drawings and samples to a new supplier. When I told him the background story, he agreed to set up additional shifts to get manufacturing rolling. We should clear our backlog within two months.*' I was overwhelmed and touched. After a deep breath, professionalism replaced sentimentalism and I said '*Great job, Thomas. We can clear the backlog in two weeks if we get the finished goods from that scumbag's warehouse.*'

De jure, it was not really possible to circumnavigate the board's decision to cease operations with this supplier but de facto procurement did get the finished goods out within 24 hours after Thomas and I had agreed on how to do it without making the members of the board lose face entirely. We asked a lawyer to supervise the selling of the goods from the supplier's warehouse to a wholesaler, who we then purchased the goods from. Believe it or not, both the lawyer and wholesaler did this for free. And the members of the board were smart enough not to ask questions how we managed to reduce the backlog in such a short period of time.

Why did I tell this story and what's the *kaikaku* effect?

'*Fear is a bad advisor*', as are unchecked emotions and cravings for revenge. In reverse order, this is exactly what led to an escalation that could have pushed the company back on the brink of disaster. The CPO and the supplier were so sure about themselves that they did not take any precautions at all to conceal their hand-in-glove relationship and their exceptional standing with the chairperson of the company.

Not even the Teflon coating provided by their raltionship with the chairperson could disguise the stench of corruption. I set off to hunt them down and end their nefarious machinations. My first few attempts to expose them resulted in ridicule and shame for me, hence the eagerness for revenge. With more than a decade of hindsight and 20-20 vision, I would unmask them differently today. My advice would be that if or when you intend to take revenge, remember the proverb: '*Revenge is a dish best served cold.*' An even better piece of advice is: Do not let your personal sentiments get entangled with your professional life. Departments exposed to external partners are always in danger of being tempted by dishonest business dealings. Therefore, keep your compliance measures fresh and in good shape so that your company never gets into a situation where it must protect its employees and/or their families and dismiss dishonest employees with immediate effect. Despite their dishonesty, some shrewd and crooked lawyers can play the legal system in a way that the company has to pay compensation for 'unlawful dismissal', which is not only a financial burden for a company but a moral one as well.

The *kaikaku* effect in this anecdote was an upside and a downside one in emotions: It was obvious from the start that the threat to abduct my children had been a hasty one and that no real danger was present. – However, the members of the board and my colleagues (even the ones who did not liked me) changed their attitudes immediately and '*let's unite against idiots*' sentiment popped up out of nowhere. – I also reverted back to professional behaviour almost instantly and thus, harm could be averted from the company. – The downside part was, and still is, if this particular dragon rears its ugly head: unchecked emotions, irascibility, thoughts of revenge, hate etc.

4.9. The COO in a scenario 2:

Easing back into a sense of normality, machines can be routinely maintained, minimum stock levels can be built up, and planned machine downtimes replace unplanned ones.

An anecdote about the COO in a scenario 2 environment:

[see also 'An anecdote on the CEO in a scenario 2 environment'] Although literature about the pros and cons of 'push' and 'pull' scenarios in manufacturing is vast, they unanimously agree that 'pull' is superior to 'push'. As soon as your euphoria about 'pull', triggered by high-flying academic explanations about its advantages, meet reality, you start musing about *'How to switch processes from push to pull?'*. You start to grumble about the money you spent on the 'Pull vs Push' books and realise that 'pull' only works if you can establish a 'one-piece-flow'. This requires you to be able to produce a single piece of your product and earn money from it. You can only establish a 'one-piece-flow' if the set-up or change-over times are SMED ('Single Minute Exchange of Die'), which requires a lot of restructuring and preparation.

The COO and I embarked on this journey and set up assembly lines in a way that WIP (work-in-process) stock at a machine was never more than one piece. Sceptics told us that the time we would spend setting up the assembly lines for a one-piece-flow would take as long as assembling the goods in the traditional way.

Sceptics hardly ever bring joy to your heart because they are usually right. It took extremely long to evaluate the correct cycle time, to arrange the different assembly steps, and to account for the different assembly speeds of workers. However, when the set up worked, we turned every sceptic into a true believer of lean management: The process was much faster. Controlling, the department of the sceptics and doubters, ran and re-ran their cost calculations several times, and always arrived at the same result: 'pull' saved, on average, 40% of labour costs compared to 'push' and cut a huge chunk off lead time.

A word of caution on SMED:

Speed costs money. When car racing began a hundred years ago, two mechanics changed tyres and refilled fuel at an average of 144 seconds. Currently, a small army of about 20 mechanics do the same things in an average of 2 seconds. The average annual wage in the UK in 1920 was about £200; the average annual wage of a Formula 1 tyre changer today is £275,000. While the process is 72 times faster, it is also 13,750 times more expensive. Thus, make sure that the significant SMED costs are justified by not keeping the WIP or finished goods on hand for long.

Why did I tell this story and what's the *kaikaku* effect?

The definition of 'one-piece-flow', where you produce a single piece of your product economically, must be taken with a pinch of salt. If you have recurring orders that need the same set-up in machines and assembly, you are well advised to invest the time and effort needed to identify how you can produce a quick succession of one-piece WIPs at each machine. A hint for those who are encouraged to try it themselves: buffer times are a dealbreaker. If you have buffer times in your production planning, you will never set up an operational one-piece-flow, unless the buffer times are technically necessary. For example, before you can pull it down the value-stream line, a paintjob must dry, an item must cool after welding, or a piece may need to be conditioned.

The *kaikaku* effect in this anecdote is an inevitable one: It is simply not possible to change a 'push' production system to a 'pull' production system with *kaizen* (gradual, continuous improvement). This task requires *kaikaku* because you have to rearrange your production equipment and assembly workstations. Your employees need to be trained on the new system. Internal logistics must have *mizusumashis* to be able to meet the new demands of the system. Besides, the change from 'push' to 'pull' is a paradigm change.

Chapter 5

There are no hard borders between the scenario 1 and 2 environments. It is more like a shift change than a relay race. Although speed is not essential, the handover of responsibilities should not take weeks but days. We are about to establish a constitutional monarchy where the monarch supervises how his subjects handle their newly acquired powers and interferes if he does not like what he sees.

Departments and their duties during *kaikaku* in scenario 1:

5.1. The CEO in a scenario 1:

He should use the interim manager as a sparring partner for deciding on the best way forward in implementing the Masterplan, which is the agreement reached by the shareholders and stakeholders at the beginning of the project – I did not mention the masterplan so far because in scenarios 2 and 3, management and the interim manager need to have sufficient elbow room for on-the-spot decisions. Besides, I am absolutely convinced that the masterplan evolves from an initial plan to a masterpiece by gathering experiences through the valley of tears, that is from scenario 3 all the way through to scenario 1.

A coaching of C-level managers and/or their second/third in command is the best approach because it provides management with the impression that they still hold the reins, and employees see familiar faces in meetings and do not have to worry about unfathomable, poker-faced interim managers out-of-the blue decisions. If the scenario 1 environment is the result of a fight from a scenario 2 or even 3 environments, then the interim manager should prepare for departure from the company.

An anecdote about the CEO in a scenario 1 environment:

Here is a textbook case about how a young, somewhat inexperienced, C-level manager in a family-owned company should be let loose and how older, more experienced C-level managers with shortcomings in specific areas, should make the best use of an interim manager/executive coach.

I was the first consultant in a mid-sized family-owned company where the 'old guard' watched me with beady eyes and moaned about the exorbitant daily fees I dared to charge (which happened to be at a discounted rate due to my sympathies for the young C-level manager-to-be). To give the C-level manager-to-be a name, I call him Carl (short for Carlton Whitfield, one of the two characters Michael J. Fox played in the 1987 movie 'The Secret of My Success'). After the executive coaching session, Carl became as successful as Mr Whitfield in the movie.

Carl and I were under considerable pressure to make things happen in a short period of time, especially because OTIF was a disgrace and customers got increasingly restless for neither getting essential spare parts nor finished goods on time.

There was so much 'low hanging fruit' that we could have made pies, marmalade, Sangria, and distilled some moonshine out of them had they been real fruit. The method we used was simple enough: *gemba* (現場, Japanese for 'the scene of the incident' or simplified 'where things happen') walk. – We walked slowly through parts of production, warehouse, assembly, and so on. After each *gemba* walk, I asked Carl what he had noticed. Like every promising student, he jotted his findings in a notebook for later review. Thus, all we had to do was amend his list with the additional things I saw. Carl was downcast when he saw the length of the list and started to complain that it would take ages to fix all the issues.

'Not really,' I said. *'It all depends on how you approach the problems on the list. If you allocate each problem to a project manager and monitor their progress in a daily milestone report, it will definitely take ages to get done. However, if you prioritise the items on the list according to an estimated time you need to handle them (in ascending order, with the quickest task first and the longest last), the items on the list will dissolve faster than you*

think. I will go for a smoke while you prioritise the list as I just said, okay?'

'I need more time for that than a cigarette break' he shot back. *'Okay,'* I said *'I might have been a bit sloppy in explaining what kind of list we need: We need to prioritise the tasks on the list based on guesstimation, where you either guess or estimate how long a task could take. You will likely underestimate the time required for some tasks and overestimate it for others. Since it's the first time you are doing it, you would have to be dead lucky to get it right. Don't worry; whatever you come up with will be the baseline you can improve with each new list you prepare.'*

With these instructions, I left Carl to sort out the priorities and went for a smoke. Upon my return, Carl had finished the list and we went over it: The first task was altering a form sheet issued by the warehouse on the parts they delivered to final assembly. Carl's guesstimation was 1–2 hours. Being over 50 years of age, when I could not find the stopwatch function on my new mobile phone right away, Carl showed me where to find it.

'I am sure we finish this task in less than five minutes.', I said. *'Impossible! Never ever!'* Carl almost sneered. We walked into the warehouse and when we had found the supervisor, I started the stopwatch and asked him to alter the form according to our wishes. I halted the stopwatch when the printer produced the sheet of paper. It showed 2 minutes and 54 seconds. Carl was duly impressed and asked to go for the next item on the list. We did that for the first five topics and, by walking to the person in charge or getting them on the phone, it took us an hour to get them done. We proceeded the same way for all items on the list and went through almost all departments.

Our approach to solve problems occupying the to-do lists for ages was the subject of discussions in all departments. Thus, we even impressed the 'old guard'. Soon, Carl and I could tackle the biggest issue, being the implementation of the new ERP system. Not only was the 'old guard' pleased, but the employees were happier as well because long overdue issues on older to-do lists were handled the same way. Naturally, dealing with such trivialities as described above should not be the main task of C-level managers. That's why Carl and I instructed the CQO to include this procedure into the Quality Management manual and audit the heads of each department to confirm they acted accordingly.

Why did I tell this story and what's the *kaikaku* effect?

If management wants to or has to get things done, it has to act. Acting immediately has the best track record concerning accomplishments. *'People who say it cannot be done should not interrupt those who are doing it.'* George Bernard Shaw remarked with his well-known cheek. Do not listen to sceptics, prove them wrong by showing them how things can be done. In a looming crisis, the manager's task is to prevent the situation from further deterioration (true to the old saying 'a stitch in time saves nine'), thus, *gemba* walks, though not only the factory but also the offices, should be high on the agenda and conducted with increasing regularity.

If, as a C-level manager, you get from the parking lot into your office within five minutes, you might count yourself lucky. The company you work for is not because you are paid to solve problems and not just sit at your desk and delegate problem solving to your direct reports. Jack Welsh, the late CEO of GE, might not have done everything right (no one does). However, he did do one thing extremely well when he said *'People must think I am stupid. I am the guy with the highest take-home pay, and I ask the most and dumbest questions.'* As a C-level manager, walking around and talking to your employees is not a can, it is a must. My wife's explanation to our sons when they asked what their father does for a living was: *'He walks around the whole day and chats with people.'*

The *kaikaku* effect in this anecdote is an impressive one: It always amazes me to observe people's reaction when they get aware of the power of immediate action. – After the penny dropped, they feel exuberant and enthusiastic, almost inebriated by the sudden gush of endorphins, about the sheer potentials of acting at once. – I am also amazed to see how fast they revert back to their old habits of non-immediate action. – I am not saying that you should always act immediately. I just say that when you can act on the spot you should do so to get pesky problems out of the way so you have more time and energy to deal with tricky issues.

5.2 The CQO in a scenario 1:

The implementation progress of the masterplan must be audited at least weekly and audit reports should be distributed to relevant parties. Recommendations and deviations in these reports should be addressed as '24-hours-actions', with all issues being resolved within this period of time, without exception.

An anecdote about the CQO in a scenario 1 environment:

How the Quality Management department can be dragged out of obscurity in a jiffy: Quality Management in SMEs has a difficult role because their very existence in a company is only due to regulations or customer demands. Even owners and founders of the company despise them for the bureaucracy that comes in their wake. This is the wrong thinking on all accounts. Quality Management, if taken seriously, is the most effective and efficient department in the company. The ISO norm is that the CQO reports directly to the CEO. Every CEO who does not use the advantages of Quality Management properly is doomed in the long run. I witnessed various examples that verify this. Demands for law and order can get certain people very agitated.

Leaving politics aside, law and order mean that participants must follow rules to conduct whatever they are about to do in an orderly manner. No game works or is enjoyable without a set of rules. Without rules and a referee, every football match, for example, would not even get to the kick-off because the teams would not agree which side of the pitch to take first. The same is true for the playing fields within a company.

One of my clients complained about the mess his employees made and worked in daily. Regular admonishments by management to keep tools in the workshop, and documents in the office, in an organised manner led to naught. Even more drastic measures like sweeping the clutter on worktops and desks into dustbins did not have the result desired by the management. Staffed with one full-time and one part-time employee in the Quality Management department at the company, which was far less than 1% of the total headcount, revealed a lot. The freshly hired CQO was down in the dumps. I decided to give him a leg up at the kick-off meeting to implement lean management. I took the opportunity of having all heads of department in one room, listening attentively, and asked

'*How many people do you have in your plant fire brigade?*' '*Twenty*', the person in charge of SHE (Safety, Health and Environment) shot back. '*Okay, and how many first aiders do you have?*' '*45*', SHE responded. '*Cool, when was the last time your plant fire brigade had to get into action?*' After a while, SHE said '*Hm, that was decades ago. Before I started at the company more than 20 years ago.*' '*I see, and how often do first aiders have to render assistance annually?*' '*On average about once a month.*' SHE answered with an undertone of 'so-what?!'

'*I see, and how many parts do you produce and how many finished products do you ship on average year-by-year?*' I asked innocently. The CTO provided the figures promptly by saying '*We produce about 250,000 parts per year and ship between 350 and 400 finished goods to our customers. Add to this the spare-parts, which amount to about a third of our annual turnover.*' '*I see, that's about 1,000 parts and one completed equipment per labour day, right?*' I got a lot of nods acknowledging my maths skills. Then I went in for the kill:

'*How many people are concerned with the quality of these parts and finished products?*' A lot of eyebrows shot up to the hairlines, or where hairlines usually are, lips were pursed, and notetaking started ferociously. As no one dared to state the obvious, I relieved them from their agony of sudden awareness by saying '*Am I permitted to assume that we have a mutual agreement on taking immediate actions to rectify this issue?'* There was nodding all around the meeting room.

'*Fine. Then I want every head of department to name one quality helper per ten employees within the respective department by not later than the end of business today. The quality helpers must have a keen eye for order. Ideally, they already at least heard about 5S and must be keen on improvements. Nice to have characteristics would be assertiveness, a good standing with their colleagues, and some basic administrative skills would come in handy too. The Q helper set-up has three stages:*

1) *the Q helpers collect three to-dos in their respective departments per week, initiated by their colleagues or themselves, where no to-do is allowed to take up more time to accomplish than an hour because they are not meant to disturb regular work and proceedings;*
2) *the head of the respective departments furnish three to-dos per week. Stage (2) starts when the Q helpers run out of three to-dos per week. Finally, in stage*
3) *C-level management ask Q helpers to implement three to-dos per week. It is important that the three to-dos are accomplished each week, it is also of great importance that there are at all times three and not five or one or any other number of to-dos to accomplish.'*

A hand rose in the audience so I gave way to the question '*Why is this number three so important? Why must the to-dos be done in a week and how are we going to handle to-dos that take longer than a week?'* '*You all know the saying that everyone can count till three, right? Three happens to be the number of items and tasks a vast majority of people can always keep in mind. The to-dos must be accomplished within a week because we should all agree with what Thomas Carlyle said* 'Nothing builds self-esteem and self-confidence like accomplishment' *and because Quality Management and the respective heads of department are going to audit the progress on these measures every week.*

If you have bigger issues you would like to handle in this frame, break them down into one-hour-tasks. It is important that your people have 'improvement' on their minds daily. Some to-dos might indeed be cumbersome and difficult to slice into equal parts. In this case, you either allocate time during slack periods, or you ask your people to do them in overtime or at the weekend.'

The Q helpers worked miracles. I visited my client nine months after the implementation of the Q helpers. All-in, they handled close to 3,000 to-dos with a very positive effect on the company. A quick review of the weekly audit reports revealed that Quality Management had not made the Q helpers stick to the 'accomplishment within a week' rule. Therefore, I asked the COO to write an NCR (non-conformity report) to the CQO by the end of the business day. To my delight, all Q helpers wore T-shirts signalling their function, and they wore them with pride.

Why did I tell this story and what's the *kaikaku* effect?

It is very easy to overlook the obvious. While fire brigades and first aiders are essential in a matter of human life-and-death situation, these situations do not occur as often as every-day work situations like planning, procurement, producing, shipping, and so on. Weigh the priorities: however serious something appears to be, if its occurrence is near zero, allocate an adequate priority level to it. Having Q-helpers is a tremendous aid in getting Quality Management accepted in all departments because they are part of it. In multinational companies, Q-helpers are yellow-, green- or black-belt six sigma experts filling in BSC (balanced score cards), analysing and crunching numbers, writing reports, and auditing processes all day. This method might be suitable for large companies, but they do not work for SMEs. SMEs need a 'keep it simple' solution.

The *kaikaku* effect in this anecdote is an outstanding one: The majority of radical changes do not last because the gravitational force of the comfort zone is close to 9g. Having said that, if you manage to overcome these strong forces for a long enough period of time you can establish another comfort zone where *kaizen* (continuous improvement) brings you bliss and joy.

5.3. The CHRO in a scenario 1:

The CHRO should prepare a list of the employees that retire, as well as the employment contracts that expire or can be terminated in the short term. The list must be sorted by the earliest date of termination and overall labour costs. Especially in Germany, this list must be discussed with the members of the workers' council and labour lawyers. As soon as this redundancy list has been agreed and signed by all parties involved, it goes to the CFO so he can update the cashflow plan accordingly. Promotions, reshuffles, as well as hire and fire decisions, are put on hold while the interim manager evaluates the workforce and takes/suggests decisions in the aforementioned processes.

An anecdote about the CHRO in a scenario 1 environment:

Back in the 'good old days', the 1990s, women were not abundant in C-level management. However, they have started to conquer the upper echelons through finance and above all, HR. In those days, women had to be much more qualified than their male competitors for a C-level job. They bordered on professional brilliance. I always preferred women to men colleagues (before your thoughts get adrift, recall the motto of the Order of the Garter) because they are, in general, more reliable and less competitive. Unfortunately, I cannot recall where I came across the following sentence:

'Male-dominated companies should realise that the principles of an organisation that suit a baboon troop (highest testosterone level in the male leader of a troop) might not be the most efficient ones for running a complex corporation.'

However, I agree wholeheartedly with it.

Charlotte, which to her detriment bordered on 'harlot', but not entirely unjustifiably so (there were rumours that she was not only discussing delicate issues with the CEO when his office door was closed and locked) was a no-nonsense, 'I-don't-take-prisoners' and above all, extremely well-organised CHRO. Thus, I was highly surprised when she appeared at my office door and announced, without much ado, '*Robert, I need your help.*' Not known for being lost for words, I could just clear my throat and indicate to the chair in front of my desk. I instantly regretted this because that chair was meant to serve people like you and me, but most certainly not the several-times-over champion of 'Best CHRO within the XYZ Group'.

I bid my apologies, jumped to my feet, and darted around my desk to invite her to sit on the most comfortable armchair in my office. Gracefully, she sat down and crossed her legs swiftly, thereby preventing a Sharon Stone in 'Basic Instinct I' moment, which told me that this encounter was going to be about business and that she was not out for another notch in her floor-to-ceiling bedpost. '*The members of the workers' council and the in-house representatives of the trade union are being difficult*' she said with a look in her eyes that could make hell freeze over. Slow on the uptake on that day, I must have had a very dumb facial expression because she added, with an exasperated sigh, '*The death list from GHQ*'.

The penny dropped, but enlightenment was followed by puzzlement: What have I got to do with that specific subject? Instead, I said '*How can I be of service, Charlotte?*' '*They want to hear it from a man. The CEO is on a business trip, and both the CFO and COO hardly match that demand.*' Her facial expression did not leave a trace of doubt about what she thought about her colleagues. '*What is it exactly you want me to tell them?*' She briefed me for five minutes and invested a quarter of an hour to make sure I got it right before she said, '*Let's get this over with, shall we?*'

I learned how a sentenced man must feel when he faces the firing squad.

At one side of the table, around 30 grim-looking people sat watching us from under knitted brows, while Charlotte and I were on the other side of the table. I was highly amused about the situation and decided to leave Charlotte's briefing aside and prove that, contrary to the CFO and COO, the CRO's testosterone level was high enough to take on a troop of baboons with an off-the-cuff speech. When I need to deliver one of my (in)famous impromptu speeches, I like to do so standing up so I could not see Charlotte's face. Her body language told me that I was in deep trouble for not sticking to her agenda. She sat still, just like an ancient Greek statue (a harpy, no doubt, was what she would turn into once we were alone). That day hell froze over. The workers' representatives not only agreed to Charlotte's proposals but gave further way to the wishes of the employers' representatives and local management.

Charlotte remained seated and the sign she made with her hand told me that I was very well advised to do so too. When everyone else had left the meeting room, she turned in her chair, faced me and said '*You are one crazy bastard, Robert. However, before you get smug, you can only get away with such talk because you are an interim CRO and you don't have to be concerned about company politics.*' Having said that, she extended her right hand so I could shake it and said, '*I thank you for the help you gave me here.*'

The meeting had been on a Friday. After the weekend, hell exploded. I got a phone call from the supervisor for the subsidiary I worked for from GHQ. He was laughing so hard that I could hardly understand a word he was saying. The gist of it was that the workers' representatives had filed a complaint against me at GHQ for my '*capitalist overtones and complete and utter disregard for the well-being of the poor and downtrodden working class*'. I could not care less. All 30 workers' representatives were invited to an incentive tour at GHQ for three days hosted by their comrades. Expenses were charged to the CEO at GHQ because he was so delighted with the deal Charlotte and I were able to broker.

Why did I tell this story and what's the *kaikaku* effect?

'*Fortune favours the brave.*' the saying goes. – Charlotte was not happy at all that she had to water down her deal to keep the workers' representatives in good mood. While it had not been her decision to water it down, her HR supervisor at GHQ had insisted on *'a bad deal is better than no deal'*. She told me this when she had been in my office asking for help. All I did was push Charlotte's deal through the plenum with a bit of an extra on top for her saucy remarks. I made sure Charlotte's account got credited for this achievement because all I did was jeopardise the deal with my bravado.

To my utter surprise, the chairperson of the workers' council visited me at home, (I was not working for that company anymore by that time) after about half a year had passed with Charlotte's deal in motion, and said *'Mr Carter, I loathe and despise your utterly improper capitalist views but I have to admit that the deal you forced down our collective throats helped the company avoid a much bigger crisis.'* *'Flattery will take you nowhere Ms A. I was a mere harbinger. Charlotte and her team did the heavy lifting and although I do feel, against my better judgement, flattered by your visit here, I ask you to be as kind as to pay Charlotte and her team a visit too and tell them the same.'* Ms A agreed to do so.

Be magnanimous in your victory. You, as an interim manager, sometimes get the praise for work done by the employees of your client. Acknowledge their efforts and share both the price as well as the praise.

The *kaikaku* effect in this anecdote was an upside one: By radically changing the agreed-on negotiation strategy I was able to achieve the best possible solution for the company. – Yes, it could have gone also the other way: down the drain. – But it didn't. – Thus, enjoy and let your high testosterone level rip if the set-up is right.

5.4. The CFO in a scenario 3:

Controlling should collaborate with Quality Management to get an update on new procedures, with procurement and sales learning about new suppliers and customers, respectively. During the previous two scenarios, it was not uncommon that such information got lost in the haze of battle. The calculation and allocation of costs have had a vital influence on the overall success of the company. Calculations should always be transparent and understandable because their results must be assigned to the heads of the respective departments for monitoring and action purposes. These actions are usually discussed in a leakage meeting where all heads of departments participate and discuss the results of the calculation. Only costs that can be directly influenced by each respective supervisor should be allocated to him, and only for these could he be held responsible by his supervisor and controlling. For example, if a company operates with a full-cost calculation and allocates heating, sales, administration, and other overhead costs to the calculation of the manufacturing costs, how can the COO influence these? He could not and would thus not care about them.

An anecdote about the CFO in a scenario 1 environment:

'Liquidity is air and profit is food to any enterprise'. It is essential that cashflow plans are accurate because the CRO stakes his life, and the life of the company, on it. Thus, cashflow plans need always to be up to date. If any department sees, knows, gets aware of anything that could have a negative impact on cashflow they have to report it immediately to the CFO. – The worst and therefore most feared cashflow effects are the unforeseeable ones. – Sometimes, but only sometimes, emotional decisions are made that have a negative impact on cashflow.

It so happened that one of the banks got cold feet after having perused our latest financial report and cancelled a credit line they had prolonged a month earlier. I got so annoyed and agitated about this highly unfair move by a bank, which had been servicing the company for almost a century, that I summoned the CFO, put him through a third degree of questioning about liquidity reserves in the company, (never in my career have I met a CFO who did not have a buffer of cash salted away for rainy days) and arranged an appointment with the board of directors at the bank in question.

The handwringing and prayer mill assurances of the board members of the bank that they had done everything they could to delay the cancellation of the credit line with respect to the long and excellent business relationship between the bank and the company, did not impress me at all. I would have preferred to deliver my message standing upright and uptight, but they made me sit down. I sat on the very edge of the meeting table chair when I announced

'Herewith and with immediate effect, we terminate all business with you and your bank. All credit facilities will be paid back in three equal instalments. The first instalment was wired when I left the company for this meeting. The second instalment will be wired in two months, and the third and final instalment will be wired in five months from today. Gentlemen (I use the term loosely) I bid you a good day.'

Before they could re-shut their traps, I was on my feet and on my way out of the meeting room. The assistant of the board of directors caught up with me and whispered, *'I told them not to cancel the credit line because I was sure you would react like you just did.'* He scurried along on my way down the stairs and went on *'Based on the figures you provided, I hardly believe that you can pull this off. However, it is going to be very tight. The time frame you set is far too ambitious. If you fail to meet the deadlines, you will have to come back and renegotiate terms.'* *'No!'* I exclaimed louder and more forcefully than I intended. Stopping at the last step on the flight of stairs, I turned around, looked him in the eyes, and said

'I don't do cap in hand. Goodbye and thanks for your concern.'

Back at the company, the handwringing went on. This time from the CFO and the chairman of the workers' council who expressed their utmost concern about my ego-driven decision. The chairman of the workers' council, who cannot meet management on his own, (trust runs deep with the comrades) called me reckless and irresponsible. There (they had been waiting for me at the main entrance) and then, I gave them an off-the-cuff pep talk in a way that after I had finished, the three worriers turned into warriors, promising me that they would do whatever it took to fulfil the obligations to the bank.

Somewhat exhausted from two emotionally demanding speeches, I summoned the CSO into my office and asked him to intensify his search for customers who were willing and able to make down payments for shorter delivery times. To my surprise, I got a reaction from him I had so far only seen in movies: he banged his chest with his fist once, extended his arm, and said

'Imperator, i morituri ti salutant.'

I know, sales need some drama to thrive, but this flabbergasted even me. I cleared my throat and tried to look touched when I expressed my gratitude for his co-operation. He was not out of my office yet when I grabbed the phone and called the COO to have a word with him right away. His answer was affirmative, thus, I set off to find him in the final assembly department. The COO was a somewhat morose sort of chap. His mood could be gauged by the number of words he used in meetings or discussions: *'Yes'*, *'No'* and a friendly sounding grunt were sure signs that he was in an equitable mood. Nodding, head shaking, and shrugging meant *'Mind your own bloody business and leave me alone'*.

When he waved as he saw me, I got suspicious that something was out of order. He revealed the reason for his exuberance as soon as I was within earshot by saying *'You scared the shit out of that pompous ass* [he meant the CFO] *and that little runt* [the chairperson of the workers' council] *with your stunt at the bank. You need all the help you can get to make it happen. You can count on me.'* He extended a hand the size of a small frying pan. I shook it heartily (don't worry, this happened well before the Wuhan virus crisis), thanked him, and told him about the down payment cum shorter delivery time strategy. He grunted and said, *'We'll handle it.'*

Why did I tell this story and what's the *kaikaku* effect?

Pushing a crisis from scenario 1 onto the verge of scenario 3 could help collaboration within the company and make changes happen faster. The reassurance *'We will handle it'* by the COO was, at the time, not reassuring at all. There was a backlog of orders such that some customers wondered whether we had forgotten about them. Before sales even thought about entering the arena to fight the good fight with prospects capable of paying in advance, they wanted a guarantee from procurement and operations that the shorter delivery times could be met.

Sales, a bunch of freewheeling con-artists, insisted on implementing a liaison officer whose task was to discuss and monitor 'quick orders' with procurement and operations as well as to report delays immediately to the CSO and me. In addition, procurement had to do its homework first and shorten delivery times, look for more reliable suppliers, and make sure the suppliers accepted payment in 90 days or longer. Some purchasers tried to go the extra mile by telling suppliers, once they accepted the outrageous payment term of 90 days, that they were 90 labour and not calendar days. Suppliers reluctant to accept such payment terms were paid only after they threatened with repossession of their goods or a court claim for their money.

Thus, with all flags flying, we managed to keep the pay-back terms I threw in the faces of the directors at the bank. The whole thing had some longer-lasting pleasurable side-effects:

1) suppliers found it difficult to re-negotiate payment terms down from 90+ days to something more customary in Germany and succeeded only if they reduced their prices, kept free-of-charge consignment stocks, and so on;
2) sales enjoyed the luxury of satisfied and happy customers where all those who made a down payment got their goods on the agreed date or before, with their OTIF running at close to 99%;
3) finances were happy that they had one bank less to deal with and send reports to, which always triggered nasty questions;
4) operations could indulge in some serious yokoten activities and the sharing of best practices, especially among the workers in final assembly; and
5) the members of the workers' council and most employees were proud that they had managed to drag the company out of the ditch.

Years later and to my surprise, when the assistant of the chairman of the board of bank directors moved in with a neighbour of ours, I learned that he had tendered his resignation a week or so after my thespian performance at the bank to start a better job at another bank. Together with the CFO and majority shareholder of the company, he had arranged, behind my back, a contingency credit line in case I failed on the pay-back terms. A bit older and a lot wiser, I expressed my gratitude for his concerns, despite deeply loathing 'behind-my-back' tactics;

The *kaikaku* effect in this anecdote was an upside but high-risk one: If you turn the steering wheel sharp to the right or left while travelling at a good speed you might end up in an accident. – The same could have happened here, of course. – I do try to forgo decisions on serious matters when I am in one of my moods but success is a fickle thing. – However, instigating a crisis situation helps to keep the mind focused.

5.5. The CIO in a scenario 1:

The CIO and his team of merry nerds are responsible for debugging non-functional and essential programmes as well as cleaning the database of obsolete, false, and multiple entry data to assist all departments in relying on the information that they see on their respective screens. If the ERP system works with to-do dashboards, IT must program automatic reminders for the laggards to keep their dashboards up to date. Should these reminders not be sufficient, Quality Management should audit the dashboards at least weekly.

An anecdote about the CIO in a scenario 1 environment:

A lot can go wrong when a company implements a new ERP system. Some of them go bust, while others, if they change horses in mid-stream, go from bad to worse. Therefore, it is always advisable to have a contingency plan. Many, especially the younger generation, forget that ships, rockets, and all other sorts of difficult-to-manage products have been manufactured without the help of computer programmes.

The company I advised was about to change its ancient ERP system to a new one. Justifiably, management was worried that the company could come to a standstill if the new system did not work.

Readers who have experience in swapping ERP systems know that there is more than one way to go about it, like keeping the old ERP operational until the new one works. In this case, the external and internal IT pundits agreed to switch off the old ERP and do whatever it took to make the new one operational immediately.

After I talked to the internal and external IT pundits, I joined management in worrying about the outcome of the swap. With the COO, the head of logistics, and the head of operational excellence, we came up with an ingenious idea to trigger final assembly with magnetic cards so they could wander with the production flow. A magnetic card represented a module where all BOMs (Bills of Material) necessary to produce that module could be allocated to the magnetic card. This allowed, and of course forced in a worst-case scenario, operations to produce the parts, and procurement to order materials, in a pull-only strategy.

Before the company switched from the old to new ERP system, we tested the magnetic card system and exchanged high fives and fist bumps when it worked. When the CIO pulled the trigger and killed the old ERP system on 31 December, the new ERP system died after a brief flicker. It took IT a month to resuscitate it, and another month to get it limping on. What had happened? The internal and external IT pundits had unanimously and publicly mocked my proposal of cleaning databases before migrating data from the old to new ERP system. One department, procurement (led by a woman of course), accepted and followed my allegory about moving houses (*'When moving houses, order two large containers. Position one at your old house and one at your new house to fill them with stuff you don't need anymore'*).

Their procurement module worked properly, but almost all the other modules were clogged up with garbage data. I had to attend to another project but returned to this company within a year when the new ERP system, along with the magnetic card board, were operational. I was not amused because quick fixes should be replaced by long term solutions as soon as possible. I told this to the COO and persons in charge in no uncertain terms. About half a year later, they informed me that they had discarded the magnetic card board and that they planned and operated manufacturing, warehousing, and final assembly only using their ERP system.

Why did I tell this story and what's the *kaikaku* effect?

However sure internal and external experts are, always have a contingency plan ready for the worst case. Even if these experts act in good faith, Murphy is ubiquitous, meaning that what can go wrong, will go wrong. To wage war, you need three things: money, money, and money. To succeed in implementing a new ERP system, you also need three things: preparation, preparation and preparation. My favourite synonym for 'to prepare' is 'to make ready'. You can go a very long way in making something ready before preparation turns into 'gilding the Lilly', and even if it does, rather overdo preparation than being caught unprepared and landing on the wrong foot. 'Preparation' also juxtaposes with the lean management notion of 'First-Time-Right' (FTR). If you do not want to leave FTR to chance, you need to prepare, prepare, and prepare again.

The *kaikaku* effect in this anecdote was an upside one: The magnetic board was a very radical change to the production planning process. Employees were only able to see a very limited number of magnetic cards and were therefore anxious that they could miss deadlines for the next orders and the orders thereafter and so on. Nerves in some departments got so frail that we were forced to print the magnetic cards several weeks before they were needed so people could see what was going to hit them.

5.6. The CSO in scenario 1:

I already mentioned the need for the sales department to cluster their customers according to some criteria. For example, they can be grouped based on the Boston Consulting Group's 'cows, dogs, question marks, and stars' criteria. This can result in a paradigm change from 'regional sales' to an 'industry-based sales' organisation. It also might require a reshuffling of the salesforce. Whether you let sales cluster their customers, or take any other step towards scientifically setting up sales and marketing organisations, the CSO has to embrace a more scientific and structured approach in their efforts to market the products of their company. The measure taken could be something as simple as a checklist.

An anecdote about the CSO in a scenario 1 environment:

The company I advised was on its way from a scenario 1 environment to a scenario 2 environment because the sales department was unable to specify the products they sold in the way that R&D and procurement required. Customers could make changes to the specification of their machines even when final assembly was underway. Not entirely with a tongue in cheek, employees in shipping told me that they already had the machines on the lorry when the CSO ordered assembly workers to change parts therein.

If or when you read this book from cover to cover, you will easily recall the importance of preparation. If not, please refer to 'An anecdote on IT in a scenario 1 environment'. Lean management discusses value streams, where the presumed waterbed is more of a circular basin with an outlet, because the value stream starts and ends with sales, from when they get the order from the customer, to when after-sales services have been concluded, respectively.

Some salespeople consider themselves to be like Jesus Christ, who said, '*I am the Alpha and the Omega, the Beginning and the End*' and some even think that they can walk on water. Between the time when the sales order is received, to the time when the after-sales services have been completed, it is essential for all other departments to have the most accurate, preferably inalterable, specifications of a customer order. Every alteration could cause minor or major disruptions in the value stream flow.

The newly appointed deputy CSO, in preparation for the impending retirement of the incumbent CSO, was eager to have a checklist for his salespeople to complete when visiting a customer, or to have it on the company's website for potential customers to download and complete online. Unfortunately, the incumbent CSO was against 'bureaucracy', which he believed *'killed business instantly and permanently'*. The CRDO the CPO, and COO, and of course the CQO, supported the implementation of specification checklists.

The CEO did not reveal his view as to whether he shared the opinion of the informed majority or the opinionated minority. Always keen on going to war well prepared, the appointed CSO, the CQO, and I created the specification checklist and ran it through all departments concerned. Due to sick and other leave of key personnel, it took us an unduly long time to get the final touch on the checklist, but perseverance always prevails.

The COO and CFO approached the CEO with the final version and after a lengthy discussion, convinced him to support the motion. Nothing could go wrong, or could it? The CSO, who happened to be a minority shareholder of the company, was still dead against the checklist, despite it being streamlined and broken down to the essentials. Actually, it had been watered down to sheer uselessness. The obstinate CSO managed to get his Pretorian guards (salesmen who he had worked with for the past forty years) behind him. The meeting that was meant to be the kick-off to implement the checklist escalated into a biergarten brawl. The CSO and his Pretorian guards were adamant of not having a checklist. The CRDO, the CPO and all the other abovementioned stakeholders kept their cool and argued logically and professionally.

This infuriated the CSO and his followers in a way that grown men in their early sixties turned into squeamish nincompoops calling the implementation of the checklist the *'harbinger of doom and death'* to their business in the short-term as well as the downfall and annihilation of the entire company in the long term. Although only a mere consultant, I took a deep breath and was about to deliver one of my infamous off-the-cuff speeches when the COO announced *'The CEO* [and majority shareholder of the company] *already sanctioned the implementation of the checklist.'* All eyes turned and riveted on the CSO. I did not like the look on his face one bit and as he asked the COO *'When did you talk to him?'* – Then and there I knew we did not just lose the battle but the war as well, at least until the CSO retired from his position and his successor could send his Pretorian guardsmen after him into retirement.

Serious verbal fights between C-level managers should never be public (especially when the C-level managers happen to be shareholders of the company) because they can have the same effect as a bull in a China shop. Even though the COO sensed that defeat was imminent, he kept his cool and asked all without a C in their job title (including consultants) to leave the meeting room in an orderly manner. I learned later that the CSO and CEO had a verbal argument that made the windowpanes vibrate and neighbouring offices vacate for coffee or cigarette breaks. All for naught because the CSO succeeded in turning the CEO's opinion around and the specification checklist was shelved, for the time being.

Why did I tell this story and what's the *kaikaku* effect?

Even the best preparation is useless if the decisionmaker is irrational. Before the reader of these lines wags a proverbial index finger asking, *'Have you talked to the CSO about the specification checklist or did you ambush him with it?!'* Of course, we talked to him and he was all for it. The problem was his fickle nature and his obstinacy to accept an, although watered-down but still useable, version of it. He would have only agreed to a useless questionnaire asking the customer for their delivery address, the person in charge of the order, phone numbers, email addresses, and other such trivialities.

There is no cure for irrationality other than removing the person and replacing them with someone rational. This story should not discourage anyone from preparing, because all participants that prepared the specification checklist agreed that they had done whatever could be done. Their minds were at peace and everyone agreed to implement the checklist once the CSO had retired and the Pretorian guard had been dismantled.

The *kaikaku* effect in this anecdote is an absent one: The introduction of a specification checklist hardly ever ranks in the top 100 *kaikaku* measures you can take. However, as above story shows, sometimes even minuscule changes are perceived as radical. And it also shows that it is almost impossible to yank people in power out of their comfort zone. – Don't bother! Keep marching on! – Time will prove you right in changing what needs to be changed.

5.7. The CRDO in scenario 1:

Depending on the goods produced and sold, the CRDO needs to rein-in the CSO to sell, as often as possible, standard products instead of bespoke ones. Usually, the sales department raises hell by telling everyone that the best running products are the bespoke ones and that the standard ones are extremely hard to sell and wonder why they are on offer. Eventually, they calm down and sell what the company can produce and deliver in the time all parties involved, including the customer, are happy with.

An anecdote about the CRDO in a scenario 1 environment:

It goes against the grain of every expert to say '*No, that cannot be done because I don't know how.*' R&D engineers are experts too. So, it takes some groundwork and a lot of convincing before they can utter those words to the sales department. My heart goes out to the R&D engineers because it is not done when they say, '*We cannot do it.*' The salespeople would shoot back '*Why have our competitors found a technical solution for this years ago?! Do they have better engineers?!'* or *'Funny, last year we found a technical solution for something far trickier than this one. What happened to you guys? Are you on crack?'* The prospect of deterioration from a scenario 1 environment to a scenario 2 or 3 environment should let R&D become pachyderms to such offensive banter.

Even if the engineers in R&D become thick-skinned or callous, it might be of no use. Admittedly, the product in question did not require rocket science to build. However, the sheer, almost infinite variety of easy-to-manufacture products could cause havoc in procurement, warehousing, operations, and final assembly. That was the reason why I asked the CRDO to stop pleasing sales with solutions for every hare-brained idea they came up with. Reluctantly, all twenty engineers in R&D agreed to repel sales and suggest standard versions as solutions instead.

However, it is impossible to have every person with a technical competence on your (standardisation, standardisation, and standardisation!) side. Therefore, sales quickly got fed up with the R&D and turned to operations for 'quick fixes', 'minor adaptations', and *'only a tweak here and there and we are done'*. This turned out to be even worse than asking R&D for solutions because these 'minor adaptations' were undocumented and irreproducible, which made after-sales service look like rabid dogs when customers wanted to have their 'minorly adapted' products fixed.

Why did I tell this story and what's the *kaikaku* effect?

Even if the major players agree with your approach, there could be workarounds that could cause even bigger problems. Therefore, either invest more time in convincing people to act rationally and within the overall interest of the company and not just their own, (sales bonuses can be a significant part of take-home pay, making salespeople fight fiercely to get them) or explicitly forbid certain proceedings for all departments. In the above story, R&D had a hard time getting all the illicit adaptations into their CAD programmes and BOMs. Operating outside the laws and regulations stipulated by the Quality Management manual made things worse and caused the company to slide into a lower scenario 2 environment.

At that point, even the sales department understood that they had to change their tactics and sell standardised products instead of bespoke ones. The majority shareholder took it in his stride and said *'We have an excellent salesforce because they are go-getters. They never let an order slip.'* – I beg to differ, selling whatever the customers want is not the right thing. It took them a bit of time to realise that. We booked the accrued costs for this experience to training expenses. Well, the notion that the salesforce was 'excellent' was highly debatable, but since he used to be a salesman himself, we took his explanation with a grain of salt.

The *kaikau* effect in this anecdote was a very negative one: Trying to stop irrational behaviour by forbidding it is akin to trying to heal severe diarrhoea by applying adhesive tape. – The efforts needed and costs involved in a 'zero-tolerance' policy are unjustifiable in a scenario 1 environment. Matters look different in a scenario 3 environment though. – Paradoxically, money is more abundant in a scenario 1 than in a scenario 3. However, people holding the money bag are usually only willing to open it when they are forced to. – Seriously, why do people have to get up to their eyeballs into you-know-what to let go of their irrational behaviours?!

5.8. The CPO in a scenario 1:

The procurement department updates their data on consignment stock, items with a long delivery time, frightened-to-death suppliers who will only keep up deliveries when paid in advance, and check warehouses for current and non-current items. Usually, an extraordinary stocktaking is required to ensure that what is in the warehouse system is also available in the warehouse. While at it, an ABC and an XYZ analysis should also be done.

An anecdote about the CPO in a scenario 1 environment:

Procurement oversaw warehousing at the company I got hired to help with their problems of recurring missing parts. This is usually an easy enough task because, based on experience, parts are missing due to

1) faulty bill of materials;
2) the ERP-system has a bug, like not all parts trigger a purchase order proposal;
3) sales accept ridiculously short lead-times, as in replenishment lead time parts > lead time finished goods;
4) miscellaneous reasons, like lost replenishment orders, overdue deliveries from suppliers etc.

However, this time the boot was on the other foot. Although this story sounds very far-fetched, it is as it happened. Final assembly complained about missing parts that led to the late completion of the final product. A quick investigation into matters came up with the missing parts being out of stock in the warehouse while the warehousing system showed the parts as available. An extraordinary stock take, starting Friday afternoon and ending Monday morning, resulted in a lot of missing parts turning up in unexpected locations in the warehouse. Relieved that the warehousing systems were up to date again, we marched on in the best of spirits. About a month later we ran into the same problem. A quick check on the inventory brought up the same result as a few weeks ago.

We launched another extraordinary stock-take and marched on as before. When after another month or two we faced the very same situation again, I got a horrible suspicion which I dared not voice because surely, I would look like a prize idiot. I indulged in some serious yoga before I visited the COO and asked cheerfully

'Did you forget to book the inventory differences into the warehouse system after the stocktaking by any chance?' The COO drew a face and said acidly *'Robert, I do appreciate your sense of*

humour, but I thought you would come up with something, anything, better than cynic sarcasm. It is not funny, you know. These monthly stock takings cost a lot of effort and money.'

All I said was: *'Please, do me a favour, and ask the people in charge the same question I just asked you.'* He looked at me incredulously and was about to launch a torrent of verbal abuse when something in his head must have clicked because his facial expression changed to a frown, then it lit up with a smile before he said *'You are as mad as the proverbial hatter, Robert. However, if you're right, I will have the lot of them keelhauled, quartered, and their empty heads on a pole displayed at the main entrance.'*

Musing about what the authorities would say about such appropriate disciplinary measures conducted in the second decade of the 21st century, I missed the first part of the COO's telephone conversation with the person in charge. Reality kicked in when I heard the COO repeat again and again *'Tell me this is not true. Tell me this is not true. Come on, this is a very bad joke. It cannot be true.'* Finally, he hung up, looked into empty space for what felt like an eternity, then looked at me and said *'It takes a lot of cheek to even assume what you suggested the problem could be and it takes even more guts to voice such an outrages hypothesis. However, your bravado paid off, Robert, you were right. They did not straighten the accounts with the results of the inventory.'*

Something told me that he had not finished, so I waited. After clearing his throat, shaking his head, laughing out loud and throwing his head backwards, he announced *'We can do much better than your scandalous assumption. According to Mr Z, whom I was just talking to, the company hasn't adjusted the stock accounts for 38 years.'* I was speechless. Certainly, the COO was having me on. He was not.

The news spread like wildfire and even the CEO, usually unconcerned about such trivialities, voiced an opinion about such shenanigans going on under his watchful eyes. The next stock take took place three months later, by which time the hand scanners for the warehouse workers were ready and the new warehouse system got set up and tested. A historic day loomed on the horizon. After almost 40 years, a company with an annual turnover in the higher eight-digit figures would have their stock in order.

Why did I tell this story and what's the *kaikaku* effect?

This story is so fantastic, that most of the even extremely experienced consultants and interim managers will have to admit that they would have missed this one. No one in their right mind would assume that such gross negligence could happen. Thus, expect the most unexpected and never stop taking things for granted. Always be suspicious. Based on this experience, the COO and I agreed to investigate further into the realms of the impossible. We found some other anomalies that raised eyebrows, but nothing as severe as this one. We informed the CQO about our findings and asked the head of Quality Management to get hold of the people in charge and come up with feasible procedures and process instructions, train these instructions, and monitor the progress in their acceptance by the employees. Never leave Quality Management out of such things because 'sustainability' is their middle name.

The *kaikaku* effect in this anecdote was a rather positive one: Some readers might wonder where the *kaikaku* effect is because taking inventory differences into account is an every-day business. – So it is, but not if you haven't done it for 38 years! – The people in charge had to figure out how to do it properly and were even forced to ask one of their retired colleagues to give them a hand in matters.

5.9. The COO in a scenario 1:

The operations department implements low-cost automations (LCA) that relieve employees from repetitive work and foster safety at the workplace. Shop floor management (dashboards, visualisations, Pareto diagrams, or anything that gives harassed managers a quick overview about the status quo) is also essential at this stage. If a shop floor management system exists, it is most likely outdated or hardly used. In this case, an instant resuscitation of it is required.

An anecdote about the COO in a scenario 1 environment:

After a brief stint in banking and international forwarding, I decided to leave services behind and focus on manufacturing by building my career working for various industrial manufacturing companies. I found it very unsatisfying in services not having anything tangible for my efforts other than numbers and figures. My wandering around in the industries brought me to family-owned and large multi-national companies. Overall, I preferred to work for family-owned companies because they were less regulated. At multinationals, regulations appeared to be carved in stone, making them inalterable like the Holy Writ. Before I let you in on the main story, I would like to share a little side-line anecdote about the stubbornness of operational excellence teams at multinationals.

The stipulated regulation was that the in-line machines had to be cleaned and maintained at every shift change. This led to tremendous waste and repeated annoyance of the machine operators because they had to recalibrate and set-up their machines after this 'idiotic exercise' so they could continue finishing the order batch. I had little experience with the ferociousness of operational excellence team members at multi-national companies in defending their rules and regulations. So, I simply changed the procedure from 'at every shift change' to 'after finishing the last batch started in the previous shift'. First, I received a phone call, then an email, and finally a registered letter with a cease-and-desist order to revert to the original regulation instantly. I did not. Only when the COO at GHQ, who was my boss' boss, ordered me to obey the stipulations of the operational excellence department (I never liked matrix organisations where the old saying '*many cooks spoil the broth*' is the very modus operandi in daily business) did I tell the machine operators to re-start the 'idiotic exercise' again.

The explanations for the sagacity of this regulation eluded me. Therefore, I apologise for not being able to shed more light on this matter. The main story is also about 'rules and regulations', but in a family-owned listed company. We produced a large variety of products like plastic parts, aluminium casings, small transformers, and direct current motors. As parts of a larger product, we produced a left- and right-hand sided 'pusher' (plastic housing with a threaded hole) and the spindles (threaded shafts) which moved these pushers forwards and backwards. Some big cheese from GHQ told operations to assemble the pusher and spindle by hand through twisting wrist movements (which caused a lot of sick-leave days due to inflamed veins, joints, and sinews in the wrist). It so happened that a batch of several thousand pieces got mixed-up where left-handed spindles went into right-handed pushers and vice versa. Naturally, due to this mishap, all orders got delayed. The head of assembly told me so with his cap in hand. After I looked at the disaster with my own eyes, I did the following:

1) I almost literary took the head of assembly by the hand and led him to the direct current motor production. He looked at me with saucer-sized eyes, wondering why I took him for a little outing when people in his department were working their backsides off to get back on track *'Did you play with a toy electric train, car, airplane, or ship in your youth?'* I asked with a facial expression that betrayed my annoyance for his slowness in grabbing the meaning of our visit to this particular department. He shrugged and said *'Yes, I did. But I fail to see what this'*, pointing at the production of direct current motors, *'has got to do with that'* pointing towards his own department. Arms akimbo and a *'Come on, think!'* expression on my face, I stared at him, forcing him with sheer mental willpower to squeeze the proverbial penny through his clogged-up thinking system. He just stared back for a while, then he slapped his head with both hands several times while he was jumping up and down like Rumpelstiltskin (a Wilhelm Grimm fairy tale, for which the head of final assembly had the right posture) with a stream of the most colourful expletives coming out of his mouth. Once he had cooled down, he just said *'Thanks, boss. I know what I have to do.'*;

2) back in my office, I wrote a memo to the CRDO at GHQ with a Wikipedia link to poka-yoke and mentioned in no uncertain terms that poka-yoke was an older technology than most of the engineers in the R&D department at GHQ could muster up;
3) I cc-d this memo with additional instructions to the local CQO and the CQO at GHQ;
4) I convoked a meeting with all operations heads of sub-departments and briefed them about what just had happened. The reaction from GHQ was totally different to the one from the GHQ at the multinational. I even got a phone call from the founder of the company patting me on the shoulders verbally and telling me to '*Keep up the excellent work, Mr Carter*'.

Why did I tell this story and what's the *kaikaku* effect?

Sometimes I feel like Don Quixote (a figure out of the novel by Miguel de Cervantes, who fought a relentless and futile battle against windmills) when I try to change senseless, but seemingly inalterable, rules and regulations in companies. However, I never give up and neither should you. If or when you can prove, with any reasonable doubt, that a rule and/or regulation is detrimental to the value stream, abolish it or at least replace it without anything feasible. LCAs live up to their names and have an immense impact on lead time and costs. In the above example, it even had an impact on sick-leave statistics because once the head of assembly understood why I had dragged him to the direct current motor assembly, he built a device with which his people could wind the spindle into (direct current position '+') the pusher, and wind it out by changing the direct current position form '+' to '-'. Most of the assembly workers in this sub-department were female. As a result, I had a steady stream of home-made cakes waiting for me in my office for the next couple of months.

The *kaikaku* effect in this anecdote was an upside one: It was the very first LCA to be implemented in any department. – It was followed by a lot more in a short period of time before Quality Management made it a part of *kaizen*.

Chapter 6

There are no hard borders between a scenario 1 environment and the end of a crisis. It is more like handing over a project from one project team to the next. At this stage, hand over time is measured in weeks. – The constitutional monarchy is established and although the monarch no longer interferes, he asks his privy council members (management) to handle matters. He also prepares for his abdication.

What happens when the patient is ready to be released from the hospital?

Before a patient leaves the hospital, he has a final face-to-face meeting with a doctor who will give him all sorts of advice about how to keep healthy and out of harm's way. Interim managers like to peddle similar advice to the management of the company they are about to leave. In both cases, the advice is well-meant but seldom well-heeded.

Management should use the auspicious time that the willingness and necessity to change is on everyone's mind by adapting the same principle as physicians in ancient China: prevention instead of cure. Physicians in ancient China were paid by their patients as long as they were not taken ill. As soon as one of the members of the community treated by the physician got sick, payments of all community members stopped. Rethink this principle to the one we live in today.

To stabilise procedures and processes within the company management has to ask the 5W and 1H questions once a year and after bigger organisational shake-ups. The results of this review have to be implemented immediately.

Who?		What?	
1) Who is doing it?		1) What is to be done?	
2) Who should be doing it?		2) What is being done?	
3) Who else can be doing it?		3) What should be done?	
4) Who else should do it?		4) What else can be done?	
When?		**Where?**	
1) When to do it?		1) Where to do it?	
2) When is it done?		2) Where is it done?	
3) When should it be done?		3) Where should it be done?	
4) When else can it be done?		4) Where else can it be done?	
Why?		**How?**	
1) Why do it?		1) How is it done?	
2) Why do it there?		2) How should it be done?	
3) Why do it then?		3) How else can it be done?	
4) Why do it that way?		4) How can it be done better?	

Once the results of the 5W and 1H review have been implemented management ought to conduct a muda (無駄, uselessness, wastefulness), muri (無理, unreasonableness, strain) and mura (斑, lack of uniformity, discrepancy) analyses and take actions based on the results.

Muda in (waste)	Actions needed	Muri in (strain)	Actions needed	Mura in (discrepancy)	Actions needed
manpower		manpower		manpower	
technique		technique		technique	
methods		methods		methods	
time		time		time	
facilities		facilities		facilities	
Jigs/tools		Jigs/tools		Jigs/tools	
materials		materials		materials	
lot size		lot size		lot size	
inventory		inventory		inventory	
place		place		place	
mindset		mindset		mindset	

If the above is too meticulous or cumbersome for your liking, at least ask every employee in your organisation

1) *'What do you like here? / What do you want to keep?'* and
2) *'What don't you like here? / What do you want to change?'*

If given the opportunity, I usually start with these questions and ask how long the employee has been working for the company to know their level of experience in the organisation. I have an assistant jot down the things that can be fixed in 24-hours, like leaking taps, blocked toilets, and so on, asap. These things are a constant bother to the people who have to cope with them, and they are very grateful to you for having dealt with them in such a short period of time.

Finally, do yokoten (horizontal deployment of proven improvements) intensively. Although not all departments are equally affected by a crisis, the departments that weathered the crisis better, or even shrugged at it saying '*Crisis? What crisis?*', might have procedures and processes that withstand strains better than those in more affected departments. These better-run departments might have wanted to share their processes with their colleagues in other departments but could not get through to them. A crisis is a wake-up call almost everyone hears loud and clear. Therefore, try again to get best practices deployed by contacting your colleagues and sharing the experiences you had.

If yokoten is not well received or not gladly given, then at least do a bit of benchmarking, which is simply 'we do that this way' as an explanation of the processes in the department without training and auditing. Some heads of department block good advice even after a near-death-experience. Some like it hot and some learn it not.

A word of caution on implementation of results:

A private enterprise is not the army. People work in a company out of their free own will. Ordering civilians around like members of the armed forces will backfire before you can say 'Jack Robinson' – Each and every employee can prove to you that your proposed ideas, measures, procedures etc. are infeasible. – Therefore, you are well advised to at least try to get the people who have to implement your ideas on board.

Should you fail to do so doom is inevitable (please see also 'A word of caution on selecting a CEO in a small and mid-sized manufacturing enterprise' in the next chapter)

Chapter 7

What to do to prevent scenarios 1 through 3?

It doesn't matter how smart your ideas are if you choose the wrong CEO and other inadequate C-level managers, you will fail. – While COOs usually sport a college degree in engineering, CHROs a college degree in either psychology or social sciences, CFOs have mastered in finance and so on there is no college degree for CEOs other than an MBA which is, almost in each country, a post gradual degree. – Therefore, extra care has to be taken in the selection of the right head honcho.

> ### A word of caution on selecting a CEO in a small and mid-sized manufacturing enterprise:
>
> A CFO as CEO: The upsides of this approach are up-to-date figures, balanced cash-flow and accurate controlling and pre- and after calculation figures. – The downsides of this approach could be tight fistedness in capital expenditures, a strict 'rule-by-numbers', an aversion towards risky projects and a general over-cautiousness.
>
> A CHRO as CEO: The upsides of this approach are human capital's importance is the same or bigger than machines, development, financial figures, and so on. – The downside could be a too social and light-handed approach towards the employees.
>
> A CIO as CEO: The upsides of this approach escape me because IT specialist are usually introverted nerds living in a different world than normal human beings. They must also think digitally. Unfortunately, not everything can be decided with a yes/no answer.
>
> A COO as CEO: The upsides of this approach are that engineers are usually no-nonsense people with a keen eye on the importance of well-maintained machines, work safety issues and have an excellent understanding of the vitality of functional processes. – The downsides of this approach could be an overly great interest

in the latest technical developments and a 'devil-might-care' attitude to ROIs (return-on-investment) time periods.

A CPO as CEO: The upsides of this approach not only escape me but the mere notion frightens me because until a CPO gets the chance to become a CEO he had been working for years, if not decades, in procurement where people are trained to get what they want, when they want it, in the quantity and quality they want it and at the price they want it. – They usually transport these attitudes into their management styles and become demanding egomaniacs with Sun King allures and Pope infallibility psychosis. – Maybe the worst of all possible approaches with CSO as a close second.

A CQO as CEO: The upsides of this approach are that the company will have its processes streamlined and straightened out, also standardisation will be on the top of any priority list as will training and coaching. In short: ship-shape and Bristol fashion. – The downsides of this approach are tendencies of these people to regulate too much and/or too stringently without leaving enough elbow room for trying something new, something untested.

A CRDO as CEO: I firmly believe that the CRDO and the CIO are in the same league, thus, refer to upsides and downsides to 'A CIO as CEO'.

A CSO as CEO: The upsides of this approach are keen eyes for opportunities and chances, a dare-devil attitude, a snake charmer's aptitude to bamboozle the opposite party with made-up 'facts and figures' and the usual characteristics of a canny con-man. – The downsides of this approach are weakness in negotiations, sacrificing too much to get what they want (actually, the CSO is the opposite of a CPO) and failing to deliver on overblown forecasts.

Whichever C-level manager gets the top job he should always keep in mind what Albert Einstein had to say on problem solving.

'We cannot solve our problems with the same thinking we created them.'

You have to constantly rethink your position, methods, strategy, ways of dealing with people inside and outside your company, and so on. This does not mean that you have to change things every day, but it does mean that you have to reflect on your doings daily and if you are sure that proceedings have to be changed, you should change them immediately. Monitor the new proceedings while the learning curve effect peters out, then let it run for as long as you or someone else does not come up with a better one.

Leon Leonwood Bean, who founded the retail company L. Bean in 1912, defined the customer like this:

'A customer is the most important person ever in this office
... in person or by mail.
A customer is not dependent on us
... we are dependent on him.
A customer is not an interruption of our work.
... he is the purpose of it.
We are not doing a favour by serving him.
... he is doing us a favour by giving us the opportunity to do so.
A customer is not someone to argue or match wits with.
... nobody ever won an argument with a customer.
A customer is a person who brings us his wants.
... it is our job to handle them profitably to him and to ourselves.'

Over 100 years later, this definition is still valid. When you find yourself in a crisis, there is probably something in your company's attitude towards its customers that went wrong. It could also be that the company had to suffer a squanderer of money for fancy buildings and/or over-the-top equipment. Losing liability lawsuits, like having to pay for damages caused by your products, can also bring about a crisis.

Muse after the crisis is over and (re)think about the path that led to the crisis. Write down the key factors to change and prevent the crisis from recurring. This is not an easy process because healthy minds cannot be changed at the drop of a hat (a characteristic usually not appreciated by wives and mothers in their husbands and children, respectively). This is an excellent protective measure taken by nature to prevent us from disorientation. Just imagine what it would be like if you had always to follow the way of thinking of the last person you talked to. Horrible, right?

Only strong impulses, like a crisis, can instigate *kaikaku* measures such as restructuring of the prevalent thinking process. Having spent years, decades even, solving problems in the same way, thinking and acting does not make changing these habits easy. Therefore, it is highly advisable to train your mind the same way you train your body. Question your beliefs, approach to problem solving, and the execution of your intentions as often as possible. Rethink your daily doings every evening to try and improve issues you find worthy to do so.

'You never change things by fighting the existing reality. To change something, build a new model that makes the existing model obsolete.' – I do not believe that Mr Buckminster Fuller's method is feasible because building an entirely new model requires, on the one hand, a lot of time and energy and on the other hand, a place or space, even if it is just an imaginary one, to erect and test the new model. I think a better and more practical way of changing things is to examine parts of the structure you want to change, apply the alterations, and return the part into the structure to see how it is doing. Whatever approach you might favour, the new model must be transparent and simple because it would then be easy to

1) understand;
2) teach;
3) implement;
4) operate;
5) maintain; and
6) adapt.

When you build a new model, build it based on One System Fits All because it will contain all six attributes that a company needs to prosper. You will have to convince many people that your one system approach is the best and easiest. You will face opposition because, consciously or subconsciously, people do not like transparent, clear-cut, and easy to understand systems as it makes them feel redundant. *'Where is the expert knowledge in operating such an easy system?!'* they will ask. Nowhere.

But who says you need experts to do every-day tasks like selling, procurement, manufacturing, accounting, etc.? You need experts in thinking and rethinking in your R&D department. Or you establish a new department called 'RETHINK' for

- Research;
- Engineering;
- Technology;
- Health;
- Information;
- Nature;
- Know-how

You will not need experts in any other department, not even in my beloved Quality Management department. There, you will need people who understand the importance and meaning of a learning curve and who can confidently say, *'Guys, the learning curve petered out. We need something new we can try our teeth on.'*

In all other departments, you need people who stick to the procedures stipulated by their respective heads of department in co-operation with the CQO and/or CEO and employees who are confident enough to say *'Boss, this is not working. We have to rethink this procedure.'*

Employees who mean well by ironing out mistakes derived from procedures and processes originating in other departments, without asking Quality Management to audit them, are best advised to follow careers outside the company or even get jobs at the company's main competitors. Seriously, how often did you (CEO/interim manager) run into a problem that had been around for ages but you didn't know about it because someone with the best intentions quick-fixed it for the umpteenth time?! Usually, you only learn about these problems when these employees are either on long sick leave or have left the company without proper instructions on how to fix the recurring problems. The employees in the departments with the faulty procedures and process are gobsmacked that they did something wrong '*in all those years*'.

They have, understandably, difficulties in realising that they must change their procedures and processes, which itself makes it so difficult to change them. In the worst case (which happens with near certainty), these procedures and processes have triggered procedures and processes in other departments, leaving you with a metastatic situation. My very good advice is to encourage employees to reveal their clandestine doings as soon as possible so you can have them fixed and turned into procedures and processes that fit into your new, one system model. Everyone who experienced the first-time implementation of an ERP system in an SME will know how difficult it is to get employees to reveal their daily doings. The biggest fear people have is to lose their jobs, to which they attach various things like their only means of livelihood, their self-worth, their standing in their community, etc. To release them of this fear is a Herculean task, requiring a modern-day Hercules. Although interim managers do not always succeed, they have a pretty good track record and can help in these cases too.

I hope that I did not miss a single opportunity in my explanations, anecdotes, and stories to highlight the unsurmountable importance of an excellent Quality Management department and system. If you have ever worked for companies with such a Quality Management department, you know what I am talking about. Do NOT take the achievements of the employees in the Quality Management department for granted. It took them a lot of effort, confidence, and, above all, convincing to establish a well-oiled Quality Management system. Acknowledge and appreciate it.

If the company has no Quality Management system, implement one!

Usually, I would recommend that this be done 'immediately' or 'asap'. I do not do so here because it is one of the most important (if not THE most important) systems in your organisation. Take your time (which does NOT mean procrastinate) to prepare, prepare, and prepare again. The first part of preparation is getting the right head of Quality Management on board. All the characteristics I could write down here you already know, like assertive, succinct, cogent, and so on, but the most important characteristics of a CQO are conviction, passion, and humour. It is much easier to awaken people with a healthy dose of humour and it will also help your CQO to survive among the renitent majority who strongly believe that Quality Management is for the faint-hearted, for people with a two-digit IQ (because geniuses need room to develop, which Quality Management constantly curtails), or for bureaucracy-lovers.

If in doubt, see what the candidate for the august position does with the following quote: '*Everyone said: This cannot be done. Then someone came along who didn't know this and did it.*' If he bursts out laughing and says '*Yep! That's me!*', you found the right person to head this department. If he is non-committal, you might want to continue your search for the ideal candidate. If you have a Quality Management system, but it is only used as an alibi, then improve it. Again, I do not write asap or immediately because it is almost impossible to fix an already rotten Quality Management system. In this case, you will need to relaunch it. If the company has no Quality Management system, find a CQO (see above), give them enough elbow room to set up a Quality Management system, and support them with whatever they need. It will be one of your best investments. If you have a functioning Quality Management system, put it on your agenda to at least maintain it or set targets ('integrated Quality Management system', 'combine it with Safety, Health and Environment', operational excellence, suggestion systems, and so on). You have an excellent Quality Management system if you combined Quality Management with lean management.

'Experience is the best teacher, but his fees can be high.' - Anonymous

In a free market environment, which is the natural state of the realm of flora and fauna, high fees indicate that you have something valuable to sell. Thus, the opposite is also true. *'If you pay peanuts, you get monkeys.'* Experience can also be something that you have done wrong all along. As soon as you are sure which things need to be changed, start changing them as soon as possible. This rule has an exception too. Quality Management needs more time to change. I believe controlling does as well, but experts in controlling should elaborate on this.

Chapter 8

Here is some practical advice to heed:

Kaizen combined with *hansei* is the ultimate tool to fix problems within a company for good. – The continuous interplay between incremental improvements and reflexions on these improvements ensure a change in company culture. – *Kaikaku* induced radical changes in procedures and processes, organisational structures and the way they are managed are prone to peter out or even to be reversed instantly once the crisis is over (and/or the interim manger has gone). *Kaikaku* measures will only last if a conscious effort is made to use *kaizen* and *hansei* to keep on going at a slower pace until the paradigm change has been concluded.

What must be done:

1) Discard rigid thinking and get ready to leave your comfort zone. Question and review current procedures and processes while being open to new approaches.
2) Sacred cows live in India, not in an industrial company. Be brave and remove whatever and whoever blocks your way to lean or change management success.
3) Encourage a 'Let's do it now!' attitude. Think of how to do it, not why it cannot be done. Remember George Bernard Shaw saying *'People who say it cannot be done should not interrupt those who are doing it.'*
4) Encourage co-operation within and between departments and boost positive peer competition.
5) Do not go for perfection in the first attempt. Implement a quick fix, ask for standardisation to prevent recurrence, and go back to improve once the crisis is over.

6) Communicate shareholders', stakeholders', and managements' expectations clearly and explain them to the people you want to fight for the good cause.

7) Train new procedures and processes extensively and ask for them to be standardised. Wait until the learning curve peters out, but not longer.

8) Correct mistakes at once! Remember the proverb '*A stitch in time saves nine*'. Do not procrastinate, act! Give and ask for feedback immediately.

9) Implement a suggestion system.

10) Do not accept false reports and lies. This advice should be straight forward enough. However, if you find yourself tempted to win some time by feeding false reports to your supervisor or a creditor who holds your nose to the grindstone, do not do it. It never pays off in the long run.

Value stream mapping is my number one diagnosis tool. Choose a large, empty wall and ask all employees in the department (for example, shipping) to show the flow of information and the processes coming into, within, and going out of the department. Allow enough time to complete this task. First set your house in order before asking your neighbours to order theirs. This means that you should get your department in shape first, then move upstream (or downstream if you are in the sales department).

This is more important than you think. Even a silver-tongued diplomat can make another person feel accused. Once someone feels attacked, they will leave the grounds of sanity and indulge in a tit-for-tat battle to prove that the fault is not entirely theirs. If you can afford it, engage mediators who are trained in solving conflicts without dealing blame and shame. Contrary to the old English nursery rhyme '*Row, row, row your boat gently down the stream. Merrily, merrily, life is but a dream.*', in value stream mapping, you have to swim against the current to live your dream and not paddle through one nightmare after the other.

Swimming upstream sounds tiring, but it is the opposite because the whole system is more like a whirlpool or a maladjusted Jacuzzi where you are whirled round-and-round. All the junk from departments further up the value stream floats (merrily because no one cares about it) downstream. Thus, all you need to do is to categorise the junk and arrange a meeting with members of Quality Management and the heads of the upstream departments to sort them out. The best thing would be to dispose of them for good or fix the procedures and processes that cause the junk to occur. For example, almost everything looks feasible and easy on a CAD drawing. However, assembly workers sometimes face difficulties in assembling these designs. Flow with your drawing down the value stream and make sure that everyone perceives it to be as easy as you think it is.

Sustainability is the direct result of self-discipline. Astonished? You should not be. Manmade tangibles and intangibles always require observance, and procedures must be followed meticulously. Imagine how long a tennis player works to practice his backhand or forehand until he can be called a professional. Without discipline, all measures taken will soon be forgotten and old habits will quickly resurface. Heed the view of Harvey A. Dorfman on self-discipline:

'Self-discipline is a form of freedom. Freedom from laziness and lethargy, freedom from the expectations and demands of others, freedom from weakness and fear and doubt. Self-discipline allows a person to feel his individuality, his inner strength, his talent. He is the master of, rather than the slave to, his thoughts and emotions.'

To the delight of my sons and clients, I have hand-outs of this quote.

Balanced scorecards, six sigma, and other such things might work for multinationals with an operational excellence department team and eager members of staff (mostly freshly minted college graduates with a *suma cum laude* degree in theory and a *rite* in experience) who analyse, evaluate, and crunch masses of data relentlessly, and then force-feed their deductions back to operations and the employees on the frontline.

I do not believe that SMEs thrive on such labour-intensive statistical models. SMEs do much better with implementing lean management. Hands-on *gemba* walks, 'just do it now!' and 'stop-and-fix immediately' measures, as well as *kaizen* will carry the company a long way without getting bogged down in crisis. Although I am a fervent supporter of lean management, I also love to de-mystify lofty ideas. Lean management can be boiled down to what parents try to teach their children. A mother often says, '*clean up your room please*' and a father would say '*think before you act please*'. A lot of headaches, waste of resources, and stress could be prevented by observing these two pieces of sound advice.

Another ideal method to prevent a crisis is standardisation. Every time an abnormality occurs in the current process, the following questions must be asked:

1) Did it happen because we did not have a standard?
2) Did it happen because the standard was not followed?
3) Did it happen because the standard was not up to it?

Standards have other advantages too:

1) standards represent the best, easiest, and safest way to do a job;
2) standards offer the best way to preserve know-how and expertise;
3) standards provide an easy way to measure performance;
4) standards show the relationship between cause and effect; and
5) standards provide the basis for both sustainability and improvement.

KAIKAKU will be back in 2022 with:

‚KAIKAKU:
At its worst

How greedy shareholders and incompetent managers can ruin
a company'

Several employees at this company asked me to write a book
about the unsavoury going-ons at their place of work and to report
about the machinations of the general manager, the sheer
incompetence of the advisory board and how their words of
warning to the shareholders met deaf ears.

Glossary/Definitions

5S: Seiri (sort); Seiton (straighten); Seiso (scrub); Seiketsu (systematise); Shituke (standardise)

ABC-analysis (warehouse): As represent expensive items, Bs are mid-priced items, and Cs are least expensive items. A computer-generated list sorted by price/item, with the highest on top, as well as a ruler and pen should do the trick with two lines on the printout.

CEO: The Chief Executive Officer, general manager, or managing director with overall responsibility for the company, both internally and externally. Because of his legal responsibility, he has the final say on any major decisions

Finance, Accounting and Controlling: The finance and accounting departments manage banks, auditors, and keep the company's books up to date. The controlling department provides updated KPIs and checks on performance that can be expressed in numbers and figures.

Float time: float or slack is the amount of time that a task in a project network can be delayed without causing a delay to (a) subsequent tasks ('free float'); or (b) project completion date ('total float').

Flow©: the concept described by Prof. Mihály Csíkszentmiháhlyi from the University of Chicago where you are so engulfed in a challenging and worthy task that you become one with it.

Gemba walk: *'One look is worth one hundred reports.'* (Japanese proverb) A slow stroll through the workshop where you keep your eyes open for things to improve and observe the goings-on, declare immediate 'stop-and-fix' measures, and ask Quality Management to audit the transformation of these quick-fixes into long-term solutions.

Gantt programme/chart: Gantt charts are usually initially created using an early start time approach, where each task is scheduled to start immediately when its prerequisites are complete. This method maximises the float time available for all tasks.

General manager: see CEO.

Ghost, or hidden, factory: This represents the untapped capacity of your manufacturing plant, being the maximum amount of additional production that can be unlocked without a capital investment. Fully utilising your hidden factory requires round-the-clock perfect production, manufacturing only good pieces, as fast as possible, with no downtime, every hour of every day. The four areas of lost production are

1) schedule loss, the time when production could be running but is not scheduled;
2) availability loss, the time where production should be running but is not;
3) performance loss, the time where production is running but it is not as fast as it should be; and
4) quality loss, the time when production is running but one or more pieces are not good the first time.

Hidden factory = All Time [24/7] minus Fully Productive Time (good pieces x ideal cycle time).

Hansei: This relates to constant rethinking of what one has done wrong and how to do it better next time. It includes self-reflexion on misbehaviours, shortcomings, and other flaws one would rather like to leave behind on the way through life.

Hoshin kanri: This means 'direction' and 'management', while together they result in *'How do we make sure we go the right way?'*

Human Resources (HR): The HR department provides all departments with enough experts in their respective fields at all times, handle internal and external trainings, as well as deal with all labour issues.

Information Technology (IT): The IT department advises on the IT-systems (especially the Enterprise Resource Planning system) the company requires, assists in its implementation and maintenance, and supports all departments in digitalisation.

ISO: The International Organisation for Standardisation is an international standard-setting body composed of representatives from various national standards organisations. Founded on 23 February 1947, the organisation promotes worldwide proprietary, industrial, and commercial standards.

Kaizen (continuous improvement process) core beliefs:

1) Humility, which reveals itself in servant leadership, letting go of paradigms, learning from other organisations, not making excuses, willingness to experiment, and reflection (hansei);

2) Alignment with commitment to continuous improvement and service excellence, long-term investment in people and community, total engagement in the transformation, and hoshin kanri;

3) Security is safety first practices, stop-and-fix measures, visual controls, 5S, no layoff policy for kaizen, andon system, two-way communication and most importantly: standardisation;

4) Respect for all individuals which shows itself in development of people, leaders as teachers, job rotation, cross training, total engagement, family atmosphere, and fun workplaces;

5) Service is customer-aligned organisational structures, pull signal, value stream design, and to hear the voice of your internal and external customers;

6) Processes have to be monitored by value stream mapping, low-cost automations, levelled workload, process-aligned frontline management, do more with less, and a continuous problem-solving process;

7) Urgency reveals itself in dissatisfaction with status quo, stop-and-fix measures, 5Whys;

8) Connection means value stream thinking, cross-functional teams, flow and visual, and visualised management;

9) Consensus must be achieved through catch ball, everyone-speaks sessions, team-based kaizen activities, and daily shift start meetings (morning market); and
10) Yokoten (best practice sharing) through benchmark tours, customer-supplier co-operation, and volunteer kaizen at local not-for-profit organisations.

Kata: Improvement kata is a repeating three-step routine by which an organisation improves and adapts. It makes continuous improvements through the scientific problem-solving method of Plan Do Check Act a daily habit. The four steps are:

1) determine a direction;
2) define the next target condition; and
3) move towards the target through quick, iterative, PDCA cycles to uncover and remove obstacles.

Coaching kata is the repeating routine by which lean leaders and managers teach the improvement kata to everyone in the organisation. The teacher or coach gives the learner or trainee procedural guidance, rather than solutions, that make the learner successful in overcoming obstacles.

Leakage meeting: A leakage meeting is a meeting where all heads of departments, chaired by the CEO, discuss the results of the post calculation of the shipped orders in a period. Depending on the state the company, weekly, fortnightly, or monthly leakage meetings are appropriate. The participants agree on immediate actions to prevent further leakage of profits due to inadequate processes in their respective departments.

Managing director: see CEO

Mizusumashi ('Water-spider'): Experienced workers who deliver materials, half-finished goods, components, etc. from one workstation to another, preferably just-in-sequence, and pick-up scrap, packaging, waste, etc. on their way back from the workstations. They ensure that production flows smoothly by receiving all materials, including information like next order papers.

Monozukuri (also spelled *monodzukuri*): This is dedication to craftsmanship, pride of what one is doing/producing, innovation, and perfection. It is akin to the German *'Berufsethos'* where a professional vow to behave morally and ethically to not discredit his profession and fellow craftsmen is taken.

Nemawashi: The process of gaining acceptance and preapproval for a proposal by first evaluating the idea and then the plan with management and stakeholders to get input, anticipate resistance, and align the proposed change with other perspectives and priorities in the organisation. Formal approval comes in a meeting to sign off on the final version of the proposal. The term literally means *'preparing the ground for planting'* in Japanese, which is what any successful and proliferous gardener does.

Obeya: This is the Japanese term for a 'big room' where heads of different departments meet to discuss project issues and track project progress.

One-piece flow: parts are made one at a time and passed on to the next process. Benefits of the one-piece flow include

1) the quick detection of defects to prevent a large batch thereof;
2) short lead-times of production;
3) reduced material and inventory costs, and
4) design of equipment and workstations of minimal sizes.

Operations: The operations department tries to produce and assemble the ideas generated by R&D with the materials provided by the procurement department, and in the timeframe and with the specifications agreed on with the customers by the sales department. The department provides frequent feedback to all these departments, as well as to Quality Management, HR, and Controlling.

OSHA: Occupational Safety and Health Administration (see: https://www.osha.gov/aboutosha).

Positive contribution margin: If a product has a positive contribution margin, it is worth keeping because its sales price contributes to fixed costs.

Procurement: The procurement department ensures it gets the best deal for the company by consulting with the R&D, Operations, and Controlling departments.

Quality Management: The Quality Management department is the 'police' department of the company. They ensure that the procedure, processes, and work instructions are followed and admonish heads of departments to update these in regular audits.

Radar chart: A radar chart is a circular chart with ten spokes, one for each of the three principles and seven concepts of kaizen. It is used as a diagnostic tool to measure, on a scale of zero (at the hub) to ten (at the rim), the degree of consistency with kaizen. The three principles and seven concepts of kaizen serve as a foundation for the systems and tools required for implementation of continual improvement and Total Quality Management. They shape the culture and thinking of an organisation's leadership. The three principles of kaizen are

1) Process creates results. Without improving processes, results do not improve. Look to improve one or more of the five inputs to processes, being persons, machines, methods, materials, and the environment;
2) Total systems focus vs. departmental focus. Look for optimum vs. sub-optimum. A penny saved in one department has no merit if it adds a quid of cost in another;
3) Non-blaming and non-judgmental. Determine what is wrong, not who is wrong. Find the cause of the problem and correct it, but do not kill the messenger.

The seven concepts of kaizen are

1) Standardise-Do-Check-Act (SDCA) to Plan-Do-Check-Act (PDCA);
2) The next process is the customer. Ask what you can do to improve products or services that you pass along to the next process;
3) Quality first. Improving quality automatically improves cost and delivery, while focusing on cost-cutting usually causes deterioration in quality and delivery;
4) Market-in vs. product out. Rather than pushing products into the market and hoping customers will buy them, ask potential customers what they need/want and develop products that meet these needs and wants;
5) Upstream management. The sooner in the design/pilot test/production/market cycle a problem can be found and corrected, the less time and money is wasted;
6) Speak with data (as Peter Drucker said, '*If you cannot measure it, you cannot manage it.*'); and
7) Variability control and recurrence prevention. Ask 'Why?' five times to get to the real cause of a problem and to avoid only treating the effects thereof.

Research and Development (R&D): The R&D department focuses on (a) future products/services, and (b) constantly improves current products/services with the operations, sales, and procurement departments but prevents 'gilding the Lilly' by standardising perfect products/services.

Sales: The sales department tries hard to not forfeit the company's future by selling its products/services with eyewatering discounts, and tries even harder to promise realistic delivery dates to the customers.

Seven concepts of kaizen: see radar chart.

SMED (Single Minute Exchange of Die): set-ups and change-overs should take less than 10 minutes, thus, SMED should actually be SDMED (Single-Digit Minute Exchange of Die) or even OTED (On Touch Exchange of Die). The exchange of dies according to Shigeo Shingo should be implemented in 8 steps:

1) Separate internal from external setup operations;
2) Convert internal to external setup;
3) Standardise function, not shape;
4) Use functional clamps or eliminate fasteners altogether;
5) Use intermediate jigs;
6) Adopt parallel operations;
7) Eliminate adjustments;
8) Automation

Three principles of kaizen: see radar chart

Value stream mapping: The value stream mapping entails the following steps:

1) clearly define the scope;
2) set objectives;
3) create preliminary current state maps;
4) collect and display all relevant documents;
5) display the current state map and encourage all employees to comment on it;
6) identify value added, non-value added, and non-value added but required processes/information;
7) eliminate redundant systems;
8) always visualise;
9) implement findings immediately;
10) audit and monitor progress; and
11) continue to improve the process.

XYZ analyses (warehouse): Xs represent either well running items or items with a very long delivery time, Ys are between Xs and Zs, and Zs are poor running items or ones with a very short delivery time.

Yokoten: This refers to 'horizontal deployment' or 'sideways expansion' and the practice of copying good results of kaizen in one area to others. Yokoten can also apply to copying product design ideas, business processes, or better machine settings, materials, or methods in general. Yokoten requires a culture of 'go see' information sharing between departments, both successes and failures.

'Some regard private enterprise as if it were a predatory tiger to be shot. Others look upon it as a cow that they can milk. Only a handful see it for what it really is--the strong horse that pulls the whole cart.' – Winston Churchill

Acknowledgments

Any mistakes, typos, etc. remaining in the book are all mine. I want to thank my clients and former employers for giving me the opportunity to serve in their respective companies. I am not an easy person to deal with at times (as my wife will tell you if you have enough time to spare) and some clients and former employers were happy to see me go. I am even grateful to them because experience is also what you do wrong. It is much easier to learn from one's mistakes than one's successes. Defeats make you humble and encourage you to rethink every situation you lived through to find out what went wrong and what you could have done better to avoid defeat. Successes, however, make you conceited with their stories getting told for the amusement of dinner guests. It is rare that you hear someone speaking of their failures. Thus, my special thanks go to the clients and employers where I could eat humble pie. I am also grateful to my family who had to go long stretches of time without me because I was off to faraway lands at the drop of a hat and returned just to get some fresh clothes and was off again to a new assignment. Last, but definitely not least, I am grateful to the satisfied clients, employers, and colleagues who would be happy to assign me to new challenges.

Bibliography

'Animal Farm' – Orwell, George

'How to Win Friends and Influence People' – Carnegie, Dale

'Creating a Kaizen Culture' – Miller, Jon; Wroblewski, Mike; Villafuerte, Jaime

'Flow: The Psychology of Optimal Experience' – Csíkszentmihályi, Mihály

'Gemba Kaizen' – Imai, Masaaki

'Getting to Yes' – Fisher, Roger; Ury, William

'Kaizen in Logistics & Supply Chains' – Coimbra, Euclides A.

'Kaizen: The Key to Japanese Competitive Success' – Imai, Masaaki

'Marketing Management' – Kotler, Philip

'Out of the Crisis' – Deming, W. Edwards

'The High Velocity Edge' – Spear, Steven J

'The Lean Turnaround' – Byrne, Art

'The Machine that Changed the World' – Womack, James P.; Jones, Daniel T.; Roos, Daniel

'The Toyota Way' – Liker, Jeffrey

www.oee.com